3D Printing Techniques and Processes

MICHAEL DEGNAN

Cavendish
Square
New York

Published in 2018 by Cavendish Square Publishing, LLC
243 5th Avenue, Suite 136, New York, NY 10016

Library of Congress Cataloging-in-Publication Data

Names: Degnan, Michael.
Title: 3D printing techniques and processes / Michael Degnan.
Description: New York : Cavendish Square Publishing, 2018. | Series: Project learning with 3D printing | Includes bibliographical references and index.
Identifiers: ISBN 9781502634245 (pbk.) |ISBN 9781502631503 (library bound) | ISBN 9781502631510 (ebook)
Subjects: LCSH: Three-dimensional printing--Juvenile literature. | Technological innovations--Juvenile literature.
Classification: LCC TS171.95 D44 2018 | DDC 621.9/88--dc23

Editorial Director: David McNamara
Editor: Fletcher Doyle
Copy Editor: Nathan Heidelberger
Associate Art Director: Amy Greenan
Designer: Alan Sliwinski
Production Coordinator: Karol Szymczuk
Photo Research: J8 Media

The photographs in this book are used by permission and through the courtesy of: Photo credits: Cover Jasmin Brutus/Alamy Stock Photo; Back cover Jonathan Juursema/Wikimedia Commons/File:Felix 3D Printer - Printing Head.JPG/CC BY SA 3.0; p. 4 Insanet/Shutterstock.com; p. 8 Joe Gough/Shutterstock.com; p. 11 Coneyl Jay/Stone/Getty Images; p. 14 Zhudifeng/iStockphoto.com; p. 20 Business Wire/Getty Images; p. 24 Courtesy Stratasys; p. 26 Moreno Soppelsa/Shutterstock.com; p. 33 William M. Plate Jr., U. S. Air Force/Wikimedia Commons/File:GMAW.welding.af.ncs.jpg/Public Domain; p. 35 Encyclopedia Britannica/UIG/Alamy Stock Photo; p. 44 Otnaydur/Shutterstock.com; p. 51 BaMic/Shutterstock.com; p. 52 Sspopov/Shutterstock.com; p. 65 Arleksey/Shutterstock.com; p. 68 Ron Ellis/Shutterstock.com; p. 73 Ahmad Al-Rubaye/AFP/Getty Images; p. 81 Michael Degnan; p. 84 Yoon S. Byun/The Boston Globe/Getty Images; p. 88 Erik Tham/Corbis/Getty Images; p. 91 Larry Busacca/Getty Images; p. 94 Rebecca Hale/National Geographic/Getty Images; p. 97 AP Images; p. 99 John B. Carnett/Popular Science/Getty Images; p. 108 Chip Somodevilla/Getty Images.

Printed in the United States of America

CONTENTS

TECHNICAL TERMS

gateway technology A technology that opens the door for the development of other often complementary technologies.

STEAM An acronym for "science, technology, engineering, art and design, and math." STEAM advocates argue for the development of creative skills that will act as a driver for innovation.

STEM An acronym for "science, technology, engineering, and math," which are subjects of increased importance for living in the information age.

CHAPTER ONE

A Gateway Technology

T HERE ARE MANY TRADITIONS OF AMERICAN HERITAGE THAT
define us to the rest of the world. These include
hard work, a cooperative citizenry that holds
individual freedom of expression dear, and the dream
of the frontier with its promise of opportunity. These
traditions represent our values of industry, liberty, and
intellectual self-improvement that were the philosophical
foundations of our republic.

The summation of these values can be seen in
another American tradition, that of inventor as hero. To
innovate is to challenge, to deny the tyranny of current

Opposite: An ink-jet printer head moves across the page from left
to right, creating words and images as it goes. This action will be
used throughout this book to explain how 3D printers work.

assumptions about what is possible. To invent is to re-create, to renew, and, in doing so, empower.

Consider the face of the $100 bill, Benjamin Franklin. One of the architects of the Declaration of Independence and the United States Constitution, Franklin was also a diplomat, businessman, scientist, and inventor. Invention is in the DNA of our national worldview, and we recognize that ideas and the human imagination are our most powerful tools.

More than thirty years ago, an American named Charles Hull imagined a what-if scenario: what if science fiction could be made reality, so that not just words on stacks of paper, but complex physical 3D objects could be "printed"? If you had an ink-jet printer that moved the print head across the width of the page while moving top to bottom down the length of a page, why not make something that could also move up and down to print something with height? This would create three-dimensional objects, things you can hold in your hand, and without the challenge of waiting for them to be hand assembled. Books have been printed for centuries; why not the same with sneakers, showerheads, and even airplanes? Hull was imagining a next step—a revolution, in fact—in the way the world makes and manufactures.

Today, you can **3D print**, and when an individual or organization wants to test out a new concept or invention, they can now fabricate it in a matter of hours, versus weeks. With just one question, "Why not try to print objects?" the resulting research produced new types of manufacturing that have been and continue to be revolutionized by 3D technologies. The author of this book has held in his hands 3D printed art sculptures, customized artificial skull implants, and titanium parts for jets. 3D technology now assists in a wide range of fields, including art, scientific research, medicine, aerospace, military technology, innovation, and entertainment.

How can one group of technologies affect so many areas of our lives? This is because 3D manufacturing is a **gateway technology**, or a type of technology that allows the introduction of other new technologies to our world as a result of its use. Another powerful gateway technology that affected our world is fire. In learning to control fire, humans were later able to develop cooking, home heating, and the fabrication of other technologies, such as iron and steel. Consider the Manhattan skyline: without the domestication of fire, skyscrapers could not exist, for there would be no steel.

The powerful technologies of 3D manufacturing did not emerge overnight. Intensive research in the areas of computer hardware, computer software, and manufacturing machine development was necessary to refine the quality and resolution of the objects produced by the machines. A comparison can be made to television: over the course of the twentieth and early twenty-first centuries, television displays became increasingly clear and versatile in size. Starting from small and blurry glass screens animated by neon and **cathode**-ray tubes,

The steel scaffolding seen here is made possible by one gateway technology, the domestication of fire.

television sets now boast image resolution that rivals nature and sizes to dominate a living room.

A broad range of professionals, from artists to surgeons, have adopted 3D technologies. However, all of these technologies were developed largely by scientists and engineers, who used logic and the scientific method to produce the software programs and machine parts that govern these processes. As a result, a common formula, or "recipe," exists to control this technology, and it will be explained clearly in this book.

How do the people who invent these tools have the ability to understand and change how the machines work? First, the inventors have learned how energy can be changed, such as in the instance of **electron guns** and **laser** beams. The inventors have studied what types of particles there are, how the particles behave in certain conditions, and how changing those conditions can lead to predictable behavior. An analogy can be made to visiting a zoo or nature preserve: by watching and listening, you can learn how the different species interact. In other words, by studying in classes such as physics, the inventors have learned how to control nature in a limited way to produce lasers.

Classes such as mathematics, biology, chemistry, computers, and physics are designed in a specific way to demonstrate the logic of the thinking of the people in history who have discovered insights in these fields. The purpose of learning these subjects in the order they are arranged is to create bundles of understanding that allow for a deep foundation of knowledge of nature and its physical laws. These bundles are also designed for sequential learning, such as algebra and biology, and calculus and chemistry.

As this information is learned through time, it passes from your active, or short-term, memory to your long-term memory. Deep processing occurs in partnership with your long-term memory, and as this processing occurs, a student can begin to see and master more complex concepts, such as the evolution of species and the red shift of galaxies that signifies the expansion of the universe.

There is an ongoing discussion in our nation about the need for increased focus on education for what are called **STEM** and **STEAM** initiatives. STEM is an acronym for "science, technology, engineering, and mathematics." Advocates of STEM education feel that there is a need for more intensive training for public education students in the aforementioned subject areas. This need is a result of an increase in jobs available in these areas, and STEM advocates argue that these new jobs must have candidates who have been thoroughly educated from an early age in curriculum that focuses on these areas.

STEAM is a modification of STEM, standing for "science, technology, engineering, art, and mathematics." The "art" in STEAM also stands for "art and design." Advocates of this initiative feel that art and design thinking and professional skills (like drawing) are integral to a balanced form of education that supports innovation. An example of this is a person who has the ability to visualize problems and think creatively, and also can apply his or her knowledge of the sciences based on his or her education.

Our imaginations can unlock new perceptions about the everyday and lead to innovations such as self-driving cars.

STEM initiatives advocate for the coordinated instruction and understanding of science, technology, engineering, and math. This coordinated instruction provides mastery of information and helps to prepare us for careers in fields like astrophysics, 3D technology, and regenerative medicine. We also talked about the value of STEAM, and how important art and design are to thinking critically, creative problem solving, and observing, which are cornerstones of the sciences as well.

In other words, science provides a deep understanding of nature and its laws; art and design support critical and creative thinking. The coordination of the two allows for new perceptions about the world around us and leads directly to innovations. This is the value of committing to succeeding in classes such as mathematics, chemistry, biology, physics, and art.

In the next chapter, I will describe a case of a mad cow. Dissect what you are reading in the sciences and liberal arts with the case of the mad cow as a guide. Identify keywords and read around them. Don't let jargon detour you, and don't fear failure in navigating the information overload of modern education, for there are guides to help you. At worst, failure can be an excellent teacher as well. Artists will tell you that in order to learn the techniques or recipes behind techniques like observational drawing, one must make a lot of drawings, especially bad ones. To quote playwright Samuel Beckett, "Ever tried. Ever failed. No matter. Fail again. Fail better."

As you push through the growing pains of homework, the finish line for you is the truth that by excelling in school, you can go to work, fire lasers every day, help create innovations in medicine that change people's lives, and design engine parts for rockets that reach outer space. Onward, to the future!

The goal of public education is to enact the aforementioned civic values of industry, liberty, and intellectual self-improvement by empowering each new generation with the knowledge and tools of thought required to understand the world around them, thrive within it, and affect it positively. This goal helps maintain an informed and educated public, and contributes to the quality of life within our national borders. This goal also helps us remain competitive as a country within a globalized economy and an ever-changing world.

Careers that utilize 3D technologies exist across a broad range of STEM and STEAM fields, from fine art sculpture and archaeology, to jet engine design and surgery. After finishing this book, you should be able to understand how 3D technologies work, what processes are currently being used, and in what professions 3D technology is being applied. You should also have a basic understanding of 3D software. This knowledge will be of value to you if you would like to explore these technologies on your own, and especially if you are interested in careers that use 3D printing.

TECHNICAL TERMS

additive manufacturing The process of building things by stacking or adding thin layers of material. This is another term for 3D printing.

CAD/CAM Computer-aided design and computer-aided manufacturing. The design element allows for the rapid creation of a drawing of an object in three dimensions. CAM uses computer software in tandem with machinery to improve and automate the manufacturing process. It can be used in subtractive manufacturing, a method in which material is cut away by drills or other objects guided by computers reading instructions created in CAD.

rapid prototyping A type of additive manufacturing in which products are 3D printed and tested for form and function. This allows for quick changes to be made in a product, which can again be printed and tested.

stereolithography This 3D printing method uses lasers to harden liquid plastics. It was initially used for producing models for use in idea, or concept, development, and now it is used for functional parts.

CHAPTER TWO

Beginner Processes for 3D Printing

S YOU READ THIS BOOK AND LEARN ABOUT NEW
technologies, you will encounter what are known
as "technical terms." These are terms such as
"**vat polymerization**" that are not commonly used in our
day-to-day lives, unless you work in vat polymerization!
The best way to decrypt these trade terms is the same
way you would deal with a cow that ran into your
classroom and started charging toward your desk. Step
1: Move away from and around the cow. Step 2: Keep
moving; you never know if there are more cows. Step 3:
Analyze or figure out where the cow came from in the
first place.

Opposite: The object being printed is produced by stacking layers
of material on top of one another as the material fuses to itself.

Take the same approach with new technical terms. Step 1: Don't freeze up; keep reading around the words, and continue reading the sentence and paragraph. Step 2: Try to get a sense of the context, or why the words are being used. In other words, think about what the author is trying to say. Step 3: Analyze the words by looking them up either in the glossary section of the book, in a dictionary, or online.

This approach allows you to read for meaning. It can be used in this book as well as in future readings. Should you decide to pursue a career in science, reading around the jargon is actually an advised technique for reading published scientific articles. This is because brilliant scientists do not always make the best writers. In having a deep knowledge of their field and specialty, they can often wrongly assume the same or similar level of knowledge among their readers.

Another way to approach this is to think of a sport that you like to play, such as football, soccer, or hockey. In all of these sports, the primary objective is to get past the other team's players and score a goal or touchdown. I find it's helpful to think of the words that I have not learned yet as players that I need to move around so that I can get to my goal of understanding the sentence and paragraph.

This is your game plan for exploring a field of technology that is being called a new type of industrial revolution. As **additive manufacturing**, in concert with **CAD/CAM**, provides new materials, inventions, and new technology, the ability to decrypt technical jargon will keep you ahead of the pack. Please keep this in mind as you read the introductory list on pages 18 and 19 of the established and **emerging technologies** in 3D printing. The technologies have been organized by the general category of material handling that is used to define the process.

Vat Photopolymerization

Vat photopolymerization is a way to coat objects in resin, a type of plastic. The process was initially used to coat paper for printing. Looking at the terms, and thinking of chemistry, "photo" refers to light. A **monomer** ("mono" for one) is a type of chemical with a simple molecular structure. A **polymer** ("poly" for many) is a chemical composed of monomers, that is, monomers grouped together as one molecule.

    Applying this knowledge, vat photopolymerization is a process of turning monomers into polymers. This is achieved by applying radiation in the form of light, from UV to visible light; as we mentioned before, this is a means of controlling the transfer of energy. Another way to think about this is that it is a way to turn a liquid into a solid using light. These materials are used frequently in denture fabrication and, very recently, in creating prosthetic eyes. In additive manufacturing, photopolymerization is perhaps most famously used with **stereolithography.**

CATEGORIES AND TYPES OF 3D PRINTING PROCESSES

Additive Manufacturing Technologies	Sustaining technologies: low volume manufacturing and direct modeling.	Emerging or archived technologies: rapid prototype and concept development.
Vat polymerization	Stereolithography (STL), Continuous liquid interface production (CLIP), 3D microfabrication	Solid ground curing, Heliolithography (Orange Maker)
Material extrusion	Fused deposition modeling (FDM) and Fused filament fabrication (FFF); Multijet modeling, Robocasting	Liquid Metal Jet Printing (Vader Systems; Purdue "mechanically sintered gallium-indium nanoparticles")
Powder bed fusion	Binder jetting, Electron Beam Melting (EBM), Selective Laser Sintering (SLS), Selective Laser Melting (SLM)/ Direct metal laser Sintering (DMLS), 3D microfabrication	Material Jetting, Selective heat sintering (SHS)
Sheet lamination		Laminated object manufacturing, Ultrasonic Additive Manufacturing

Additive Manufacturing Technologies	Sustaining technologies: low volume manufacturing and direct modeling.	Emerging or archived technologies: rapid prototype and concept development.
Directed energy deposition	Electron beam freeform fabrication (EBF3) by NASA, Laser Engineered Net Shaping (LENS), Laser Powder Forming	
Concrete and stone construction 3D printing		Contour Crafting, D-Shape
Microprinting		Microscale metamaterials, Projection micro-stereolithography
Biotechnology AM	Tissue Engineering, Organs on a chip, Wake Forest's Integrated Tissue and Organ Printing System (ITOP), Organovo, Printing collagen	Magnetically assisted slip casting
4D Printing		Self-assembling 3D printing materials

Stereolithography, once limited to a very few colors, has evolved to use a wide range of colors and textures.

Stereolithography (SLA)

Stereolithography was invented by Charles Hull in the 1980s when he realized that photopolymerization layers could be stacked on top of one another to form shapes. The first 3D print he created was a small cup. Think back to the original description of the ink-jet printer printing words from left to right (x axis), and sentences from the top of the page to the bottom (y axis). The reason we have recalled the image of the desktop paper printer is that stereolithography took that exact approach and added stacking, or the *z* dimension.

Despite the broad applications for 3D printing now, at the time of its invention it was difficult for potential customers to understand the value of the product. Eventually people understood the value of stereolithography for what is now known as **rapid prototyping**. Today, the company Hull founded to provided stereolithographic models and machines, 3D Systems, is one of the largest 3D printing companies in the world.

Hull's invention was adopted for the use of producing models to represent early-stage concepts, or prototypes. In manufacturing, a single-run custom-made object used to be prohibitively expensive, in contrast to a large-run group of objects that are made from the same pattern. As a result, prototypes were also very expensive, despite being an integral part of the invention and product improvement process. One clear value of rapid prototypes made by stereolithography was the way in which the printers could produce custom-manufactured parts at a relatively low cost.

After a stereolithographic model emerges from the printer, it still requires some treatment, or post-processing, also known as finishing. This quality can be seen as a disadvantage as the model is not immediately ready for use. However, the surface of a stereolithographic object can be easily modified, allowing it to be customized for final use.

Continuous Liquid Interface Production (CLIP)

At a TEDx talk in 2015, Joseph DeSimone, a co-inventor of CLIP, displayed an object behind him that was 3D printing while he spoke. The presentation was very effective as the object was raised slowly out of a liquid pool of resin, much like the imagined technology in *Terminator 2*. CLIP builds on the methods used by SLA by exposing liquid resin to UV light to photopolymerize it. However, whereas stereolithography builds up models sequentially in layers, CLIP works continually, and therefore faster. What made the demonstration of CLIP so striking were two qualities: first, the speed at which the object was printed; and second, that the object was printed upside down.

The first is actually a result of the second, and both are intentional. CLIP was invented in direct response to SLA technology, and the innovations added to CLIP were developed in response to what Carbon, the company that produces CLIP, refers to as SLA's limitations or "bugs." SLA is not continuous in its production; it is sequential, with the resin deposited and cured in a series of steps, much like a **ziggurat**. This adds time to production, according to Carbon, and by curing the resin into the shape of the object directly within the pool of resin, the process is sped up. This allows for another element of production to be directly controlled: time.

How many times have we heard the phrase "time is money"? In industry, this translates to the effect that a delay in production can have on profit. SLA has improved the turnaround time for modeling, as we discussed earlier, when we learned about rapid prototyping. Carbon aims to change the field of additive manufacturing by speeding up the making process by two orders of magnitude. The advertising the company uses to present its product also touches on a critical point in both 3D printing and this book. The current abilities of additive technology now allow for reliability in functional parts— i.e., parts that can be used for their designed purpose, rather than represent a part to be made later.

This speed is not unique to CLIP. However, it is a powerful selling point for CLIP or any direct modeling technology as it reduces time from concept to sales. This type of speedy making, or production ability, allows a company using direct modeling to react rapidly to new ideas and inventions, bring them more quickly to market, bring new research developments to medicine, and adapt to market challenges. This extends outward into the economy of a whole nation, and even the entire world, as adaptability allows an economy to react to economic problems, such as a banking crises or the closing of steel factories, more quickly. This is discussed further in chapter 5, in the section on business and innovation.

Material Jetting

Material jetting involves the use of a printed model and simultaneously printed supports; imagine a building

Advances in 3D technology allow users to produce multimaterial objects, such as these bike helmets made on a Stratasys printer.

and scaffold built together. This process is an excellent example of the analogy to a two-dimensional printer. Of all the processes described in this book, material jetting is the closest to ink-jet printing.

Material jetting does not use finished material that is melted or re-formed as it is extruded. Instead, droplets are delivered from a nozzle onto a platform. The nozzle is controlled by a robotic arm that moves in three dimensions. The material is built sequentially in layers, and cured using UV light. One of the more interesting features of this technology is that different materials with similar properties can be printed together to create an object with different features, such as varying types of texture and color. This is a further contribution to direct modeling, as opposed to creating a rapid prototype.

Waxy support structures can be washed away with a waterjet, a machine with a high-pressure water hose and nozzle (for aiming) and a splash shield. This machine is a lot of fun to use, like a mini–car wash, having used one myself during my education. After the support structures are washed away, the remaining object (in my case, a plastic model of the floor of an eye socket made from CT data) needs little post-processing treatment. Some machines even allow the utilization of the wax as build material, a feature that is useful for jewelry design and investments, where metal is poured into a plaster mold holding a wax model, and the wax is burned out and replaced by the metal.

Binder Jetting

Binder jetting produces models with highly detailed textured and colored surfaces that are made of plaster. The logic of the printing process is the same as the aforementioned technologies, having been developed largely in the 1990s, first at MIT and later commercially by Z Corp. The keyword in understanding this technology is "binder": the platform will have particles in the form of powder on it that are then fused together using a binding agent.

The material is organized, cured, and then stacked sequentially to fabricate the model. In other words, the

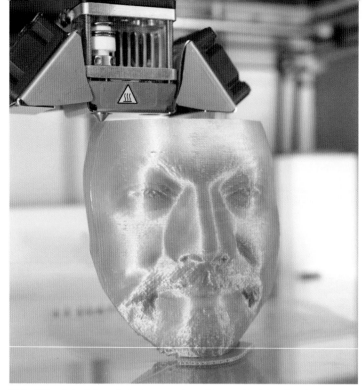

This 3D-printed face is being produced by material extrusion; a filament of material is sent through a heated printer nozzle and deposited sequentially in layers. Each layer is contoured in a way that, when stacked, produces a model of a human face.

math is similar, but the chemistry is different in regards to how the technology operates. One of the advantages of this process is the detail of imagery and breadth of color palettes that are able to be used, creating a visually attractive and higher-resolution surface. The coloration and detailing are done as the model is built, allowing for high-resolution printing, such as a photo of a face. This process is helpful in creating good-looking models quickly.

As mentioned before, part of the innovation here is the material used: plaster. If you have ever seen plaster cracking, whether in a home due to water damage or indoor football, or in a dropped, small statue, you can understand the limitations involved. You can't drive a plaster car very easily! However, I have seen this technology create very beautifully colored and surprisingly high-resolution busts of people's heads. When it comes to representation (as opposed to rugged durability), this technology shines.

Material Extrusion

There are several types of material extrusion, some of which you have probably heard about. If you have heard the names Stratasys, RepRap, and MakerBot, and seen machines extruding brightly colored filament, then you have seen material extrusion in action.

This approach uses similar logic to a heated glue gun. Printing material, such as plastic, is pushed (or **extruded**) through a nozzle that moves left to right and front to back (x and y axes) to lay down material. The platform moves in the z axis. The new material being added to the model bonds easily with the previous layers as it is the same chemically.

Similar to stereolithography, a model is fabricated layer by layer, as opposed to CLIP. The fusion between layers occurs because it is all the same material. In other words, when the molten material makes contact with the cooler but same material, it has no problem bonding.

This approach to 3D printing provides an opportunity for discussing intellectual property. Pioneered by the company Stratasys in the 1980s, the name "fused deposition modeling" is trademarked, meaning that it cannot be used by other companies for their version of the same type of printer. The company RepRap, motivated by the open-source community, created machines that use the same methods under the name "fused filament fabrication," or "FFF," to allow the technology to be adopted and rapidly improved upon by a larger, global home-user community.

An analogy can be made between Stratasys and RepRap to Microsoft Windows and Linux. The latter group is comprised of operating systems for computers, allowing users to run software programs such as Microsoft Word. The open-source community's position is that this technology is overpriced, and by preventing public access, Microsoft is discriminating against lower-income users (such as the third world) as well as inhibiting technological innovations. Linux was created as an alternative operating system that uses programs that permit very similar functions, such as word processing, but are available for free download and sharing.

Linux now has a global community of users, and there are many alternative open-source programs, such as Libre Office, that allow anyone with a PC or laptop to create similar results and open or modify the same file type, such as a .docx. Similarly, RepRap allows users to print with, as well as print repair parts for, its home machines. In other words, RepRap machines can help print whole RepRap machines.

Fused Filament Fabrication (FFF)

RepRap also accelerated the availability of relatively inexpensive machines, allowing increased access to the technology by a larger audience of users, eliciting similar results as Linux. By providing machines that can self-replicate their own parts for repair or production of new machines, RepRap has also reduced costs for repair. Furthermore, because of the durability of the plastic used, RepRap and other similar machines, such as MakerBot and Cube devices, can be used for home repair. Examples of products that can be manufactured for use in the home include showerheads and hardware such as drawer handles.

This is an example of how innovations in the field of 3D printing have led to changes in the industry. The advent of printers with relatively high accuracy and low cost has resulted in the emergence of different types of low-cost printers (i.e., competition) as well as the ability of the machine user to save money on home costs. Much like the argument for freeware like Linux and Libre Office, the open-source movement might argue that democratizing technology allows for economic empowerment for users from different backgrounds. The counterargument that could be made by companies such as Stratasys is that they need to recoup their initial investment in research costs over years. We will also encounter this issue later when we discuss selective laser sintering.

To further illustrate the effect of open-source development of FFF technology, as of this publishing, there are more than two hundred companies offering FFF printers listed on the website http://www.3ders.org. Many of these are for the hobbyist and home market. While the technology for different FFF printers is generally the same with regards to approach–e.g., a chassis or body with joint stabilization, a platform, and an extruder unit containing a nozzle–there are many variations to printer design and to part specifications, such as nozzles.

The unifying element of these designs, in addition to the aforementioned list, is the fact that they use a filament that is already in a solid state before being heated and extruded, or sent through the nozzle. This therefore classifies them also as solid-state additive manufacturing technologies.

In 2013, the company 3Doodler brought an innovative approach to extrusion printing by creating a handheld 3D printer. The company's team took the extruder unit and removed it from the printer box, allowing the user to "draw" and print in the air. While there may be a trade-off in resolution, speaking personally, there is a tremendous gain in versatility.

As an artist, it is very rewarding to be able to 3D print expressively, with no interference between myself and the printed result, or sculpture. The step of using CAD software necessitates a level of planning that can restrict the user (artist) in his or her expressive gesture. This can be frustrating or even counterproductive to the creation of art.

Also, in my experience with teaching CAD to artists, CAD software often (but not always) is designed from the ground up with the language of engineers and computer programmers. In other words, the artist user is trying to use a tool designed for another purpose. The value of the handheld printer for the artist is that it opens the door to rapid and direct modeling via the artist's imagination.

Liquid Metal Jet Printing (Vader Systems)

Vader Systems was founded in Buffalo, New York, by Scott and Zack Vader to develop an innovative approach to 3D printing that utilizes printing materials that can be found in the hardware store to create high-precision printing of liquid metal. The printing head action is similar to our old friend the ink-jet printer in that it operates on the x, y, and z axes, delivering drops of the material to desired locations.

The printing technology itself is simple but highly scientific in its method. An aluminum wire is fed within the printer head through a ceramic nozzle. An electromagnetic coil is wrapped around the nozzle. Remember in chemistry or physics class when you were shown how to create an electromagnet by attaching a copper coil to a battery? The same phenomenon occurs here. When the electromagnetic coil is activated with electricity, it produces a magnetic field to send out, or jet, drops of liquefied aluminum. Each time the magnetic field is active around the printer head, it forces out the liquid metal on the desired location. Drop after drop is added sequentially in layers, at a rate of one thousand times per second, to build custom metal parts.

Powder Bed Fusion

The keyword to understanding this process is "fusion." **Powder bed fusion**, or PBF, utilizes powdered material that can be fused, or welded together, by a heat source. A model or part is built using this method by applying layer upon layer of material, and heating the powder so that it fuses to the previous layer. This method is a variation on the theme that we have been encountering. Specifically, there is a photo- or thermal-induced change in material, material is added layer by layer, and the material is melted to itself.

PBF is actually a family of technologies that use similar approaches. Considering the analogy of an evolutionary tree, some of the branches sprouted earlier than others, and some are more suited to specific tasks or environments than others. This can be seen in the case of electron beam melting (EBM), which produces a quality of model high enough to be included in medical applications.

Manual welding in the twentieth century involved MIG and TIG welding, forerunners of the automated, precise forms used today.

PBF also can use a broad variety of materials because of the design of the technologies: virtually any material that can be powdered and melted to itself can be used, including metals like steel, titanium, aluminum, and copper. As mentioned before, I have held materials used and produced by this method. The titanium powder that would eventually fly thousands of feet in the air as an airplane part was stored in a humble jar, which was also surprisingly heavy.

The machined structural part (which is different from a prototype model) produced out of the titanium powder that I held just after it was printed was a strut for an airplane produced out of the titanium powder. You could see the lines of layering and feel the strength of the metal in the part. I was surprised to learn that at that time the parts produced by this process sometimes needed evaluation after manufacturing because there might be pores or bubble-like spaces within the material as a result of the process. These pores could spontaneously fracture during use, and that is not ideal at 30,000 feet (9,114 meters). The parts were scanned using a CT machine to allow for internal examination.

Electron Beam Melting

Electron beam melting is a proprietary technology–that is, a technology that cannot be used without the knowledge or permission of the owner. EBM is the brainchild of Arcam, a company from Sweden that has since been acquired by General Electric (GE). While technologies such as powder bed fusion use lasers to heat materials, EBM uses an electron gun to heat the contents of the build chamber. An electron gun shoots a concentrated stream of electron particles at a given target, such as powdered titanium.

How is an electron gun different from a laser? An electron gun uses electrons to form a stream or beam; a laser concentrates and sends out a beam of photons to

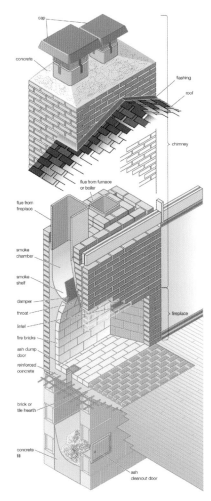

An analogy for controlling gases and heat in build chambers is the fireplace and flue in many homes.

heat the target. Both of these instruments exist on their own as tools, outside the field of 3D printing. Additive manufacturing machines can also be thought of as coordinated assemblies or functional constellations of tools.

One of the key points advertised for EBM is the density of the metal parts that are made by the melting of the metal into "pools." This means that the electrons that are being shot at the metallic powder are transferring enough energy that the titanium metal changes from a solid to a liquid. This is a very different process from welding and sintering, as we will see later. However, EBM also uses an electromagnetic coil to control the melting process.

Some of the technologies mentioned in this book also use special conditions in the build chamber to affect the temperature as well as control how the energy is affecting the material. An older but effective example of this is the development of the fireplace and the flue. The flue of a fireplace controls how much air is moving up the chimney.

This is actually chemistry at work: the flue helps to regulate and control how much oxygen is being fed through the flames, making them hotter or cooler. The design controls the air around the energy reaction, further regulating the event. Similarly, in EBM, the build chamber utilizes vacuum technology, while in other forms of AM the gases may include argon or nitrogen.

The rapid development of a variety of different 3D printing technologies in the last thirty years has emerged in part due to a commitment and interest in improving and modifying the subcomponents of the machines, such as the heating elements. If we look at EBM and the laser technologies, there are several innovations and modifications to the elements of manufacturing: the heating element (such as laser and electron beam); the state of material used (solid and powdered); the material delivery method (hoppers or trays and rollers); and the gases used inside the build chamber.

The Laser Group of PBF Technologies

In addition to EBM, PBF includes several laser-based technologies: selective laser sintering (SLS), selective laser melting (SLM), and direct metal laser sintering (DMLS). Now, it's pretty much accepted that lasers are awesome. However, we want to think critically and say yes, lasers *are* awesome, but why are we using them? Think back to the first chapter when we discussed the domestication of fire. Why did our ancestors risk life and limb to build fire pits, which led to hearths, fireplaces, and now in-floor heating? The immediate benefits of the domestication of fire included warmth, or control of environment; increased safety; and better nutrition because of more easily digested cooked foods.

The long-term benefits included the emergence of new technologies via new materials such as copper, iron, and steel. But how did these new (to us) materials emerge? The materials were modified by the heat of the fire. In other words, our ancestors were able to find new levels of control over their environments by heating these materials at specific levels for a given amount of time. In the example of iron, this occurred very naturally, as iron exists in dirt as iron ore.

The keywords here are "material," "control," "environment," and "time." We can also think of fire in the context of its properties: it is a plasma, or a state of matter that produces the transference of energy, such as heat. Heat is the excitation of electrons, and (remember the electron gun) the transference of electrons causes a change in the properties of a material.

For our ancestors, control of heat meant the ability to have roasted potatoes instead of cold ones, which can be truly gross to eat. The evolution of our knowledge of the transference of energy and how to heat materials now allows us to heat artificially created plastic polymer powders with lasers to the point where the material properties change. The key point of change for these powders is what is called the glass transition point, or temperature. This point refers to when the material changes from an inflexible plastic to a more rubbery one. The heating of the polymer powder to the glass transition point allows it to merge without turning into a liquid.

For selective laser sintering, the build chamber is heated as well to create the ideal conditions for this to occur. The "selective" in selective laser sintering refers to the usage of the laser. Instead of blasting or heating the entire tray of powder at once, the laser is instructed to carefully and precisely sinter specific particles together. This is the entrance of the use of the glass transition point: the laser is used to allow the particles to attach themselves to one another, and in doing so, change state.

Selective laser sintering is one of the most commonly used forms of PBF 3D printing. It was invented in 1989 at the University of Texas by then student Carl Deckard and one of his professors, Dr. Joe Beaman. It was patented and developed for commercial use by Dr. Deckard's company, DLM; DLM was later acquired by 3D Systems. The patent has expired, and now there is broader commercial development of the technology, including for home use. Think back to FDM and the transition from strictly research to patenting and large-scale commercial success. This was followed by a transition to an open-source state of intellectual property, and then accessibility for the hobbyist and home user, including artists.

The trick with SLS for home use will be the safe control of lasers and the heating of the build chamber. The average home user is relatively familiar with using heated tools, such as glue guns, heat guns, and welding torches. FDM and FFF had an easier time transitioning to the home market as a result. Lasers may present a different challenge.

The powders used by SLS are primarily plastics, but they can be made up with a variety of combinations of materials, such as aluminum powder and glass. These allow for a range of properties from ruggedly hard to rubbery to waxlike. If you have heard of machines that can 3D print sneaker prototypes, this is an example of that. This versatility, combined with the ability to produce stable complex geometric shapes with support structures explains the popularity of SLS as a direct modeling technology. One use of this versatile technology is for customized prostheses. This breadth and reliability of industrial use by a variety of professions would categorize this technology as a **sustaining technology**, as opposed to an emerging technology.

Totally Metal

Selective laser melting (SLM) and direct metal laser sintering (DMLS)–also known as laser melting and laser cusing–are frequently described as interchangeable terms for the same process. Primarily developed in Germany, these processes are described as having interchangeable names due to differences in intellectual property in commercialization–a recurrent theme in technology commercialization. Think back to FDM and FFF, and the importance of names in the marketplace.

A good way to understand these processes (for the sake of simplicity, we'll use the term SLM) is to look at the material transformation (heating) process and how the materials are changed. First, the materials themselves are different, primarily metals instead of plastics. This includes copper, iron, cobalt chrome, aluminum, and stainless steel. During SLS, the plastic particles are merged using a very specific temperature point that allows the particles to merge without fully melting. During SLM, the metal powder particles are fully melted in order to create a total metal mass or object with a relatively uniform structure.

The industries that currently make the most use out of this sustaining technology require customized metal parts with a high level of reliability, meaning that if the parts fail, very bad things happen. The industries also need new and often innovative complex shapes (geometries). In industrial-scale production, a small run can lead to very high costs. While the current costs of production for SLM parts are relatively high, that is due more to the time involved in producing them. The industries that use SLM for production are able to accommodate higher-ticket items in their budget.

Have you guessed what these industries are? The aerospace and medical industries are a good match for this technology based on their needs for customization and also innovation. In aerospace, there is a continual push for competitive innovation to be faster and better; however, there is an equal need for reliability. As mentioned before, the need for reliability is essential in aircraft, flight, and space exploration, for when metallic aircraft components fail, the aforementioned very bad things can happen. The consequences can be high, both in human cost and dollar figures.

Similarly, but with a slightly different performance focus, the field of medicine by its nature necessitates that technologies used in treatment of our bodies for injury and illness be safe and reliable. A vow to "do no harm" is part of the Hippocratic oath, which is part of the foundation of medical care. Part of that care includes the repair or protection of parts of our anatomy, such as our leg bones, which are connected to our hip bone and serve an important function.

At times the need arises for those bones to be replicated in titanium, for the sake of safety. This is where the ability of SLM to create customized metal parts with complex shapes also shines, as our bodies can be very complex in terms of contour. Anyone who has tried to draw a portrait can attest to this. SLM can produce a customized replacement body part to be surgically placed inside the body, or implanted, with the knowledge that this implant has a high level of structural integrity by the way it was 3D printed, i.e., melted together.

Finally, in thinking of PBF technologies, a good identifier is the use or nonuse of lasers. Like EBM, selective heat sintering (SHS) uses a non-laser heat source via a thermal (heated) printer head that is used to melt the powdered material (such as plastic) together. Despite being awesome, lasers use a lot of energy, and so one of the advantages of SHS is that it uses less energy due to its type of fusion, the thermal printer head. However, SHS is not used for functional parts; instead, it is regularly used for prototypes, and this temporary limitation would classify it as an emerging technology.

Emerging and Future Technologies

Lamination technologies refer to both laminated object manufacturing (LOM) and ultrasonic additive manufacturing (UAM). Both of these technologies use material in the form of sheets that are stacked and bonded together, and then finished to the desired shape. LOM uses paper that is glued together in layers and then cut. UAM uses metal sheeting that is ultrasonically welded.

These technologies are creative approaches to similar themes in 3D printing: building by layer; merging material together by an external source, either chemical or energy bonding; and post-processing finishing, through cutting or CNC milling, respectively. Remember the introduction to stereolithography that described the origins of vat polymerization: the processing of resin coatings on paper. Now fast-forward to these technologies and you can see that many of the materials are shared, but a great deal of creative thinking has gone into the evolution of technologies.

Few areas of 3D printing have created as much attention and discussion as **biotechnology AM** and, in the area of organ transplant treatment, **organ printing**. The controversy and promise of organ printing is discussed further in chapter 4. In the table of 3D technologies at the beginning of this chapter, there are many other types of specialized and new technologies that are there for further reading on your own. This includes the exciting applications of self-assembling 3D printing, known as **4D printing**, as well as the printing of concrete for home construction and space exploration.

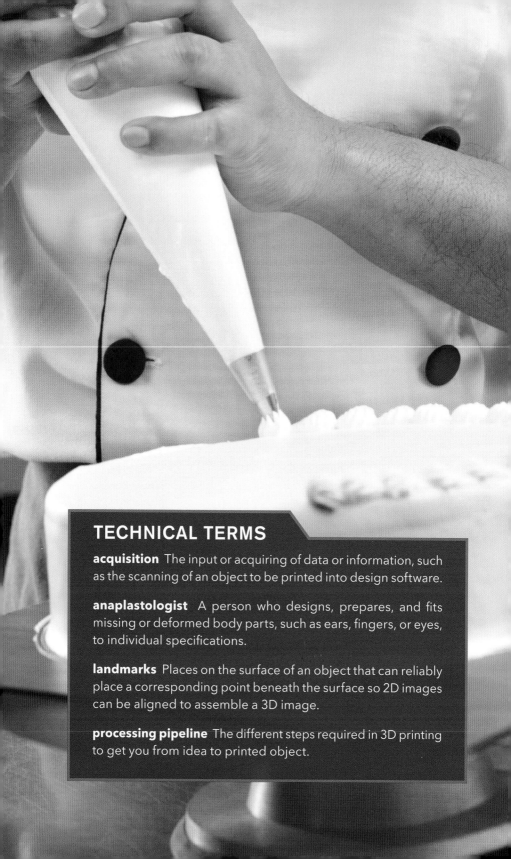

TECHNICAL TERMS

acquisition The input or acquiring of data or information, such as the scanning of an object to be printed into design software.

anaplastologist A person who designs, prepares, and fits missing or deformed body parts, such as ears, fingers, or eyes, to individual specifications.

landmarks Places on the surface of an object that can reliably place a corresponding point beneath the surface so 2D images can be aligned to assemble a 3D image.

processing pipeline The different steps required in 3D printing to get you from idea to printed object.

CHAPTER THREE

The Processing Pipeline

THE PURPOSE OF THE PREVIOUS CHAPTER WAS TO familiarize you with the broad range of applications of 3D technology by reading a survey of some of the types of 3D printing that you can use. In this chapter, we will look under the hood of the overall 3D printing process, with the goal of providing you with a deep understanding of how this technology works.

There is a simple formula called the **processing pipeline** that is shared by all different kinds of 3D technology, from laser scanning, to modeling software programs, to laser sintering. Once you understand the pipeline and its formula, you can learn

Opposite: The processing pipeline can be used to describe the role of printing in 3D technology. The pipeline is easily understood using the analogy of baking a cake.

about the technologies more easily, and you can control them as well. The pipeline can be described with the following words: input, processing, output, and post-processing or finishing.

I have used the following analogy many times for many different audiences, from college students to people in their seventies. I am confident it will be of use to you because the analogy I use is a dessert, and so many of us love cake. Now, think of when you want to make a cake. You assemble the ingredients, measure them, mix them together, and then put the batter in the oven. The batter is then baked using heat over time, and then taken out of the oven. You apply icing, perhaps even a few marzipan flowers, light the candles, and voila! Happy birthday Grandma!

The processing pipeline is best understood using this cake analogy: input for mixing, processing for baking, output for taking the cake out, and finishing for icing. It is worth noting that, as of the writing of this book, computers are not sentient. They are only able to produce objects (or "output," or cakes) based on the quality of the ingredients that are put in. In other words, if the computer is given bad instructions or a poorly made model during the beginning of the "baking" process, then the resulting print will not be accurate. Bad ingredients equal bad baking and, even worse, bad cake.

These concepts will be expanded upon below, and by the end of this chapter you should have a more clear understanding of what goes on inside of 3D technologies and how to get the best out of them. One of the first steps in becoming a master chef is learning to follow the recipe (until you can improve it!).

Key Concepts: *x, y,* and *z* Axes

The first step in learning the AM recipe is to see how the ingredients are assembled. The best way that I have learned to organize the steps involved in generating a 3D computer model is to recognize that we are designing an object in three-dimensional space: left and right, up and down, forward and backward. Another way to say this is width, height, and depth, which is what we are doing when we measure an object—say, a box of crackers, or, even better, a box of candy. Clearly, I was writing this chapter when I was hungry.

For those of us who like math, this next part correlates what you have learned or are learning with the overall making process. In algebra class, we learned about the x and y axes; this is our roadmap to understanding how 3D printing, 3D scanning, and 3D software are designed and can be controlled. In other words, this is one of the most powerful tools that you can use to learn to control 3D technology.

We also learned about the z axis, or the imaginary arrow coming out of the page, adding dimension to algebra and leading to the geometry of 3D shapes. This could also be described as forward and backward, or depth. This is the three in 3D, and it is this depth

HOW I LEARNED CAD/CAM

This book is written for a broad range of students and skill levels. It is one of my goals to help students and readers see the value of learning algebra, math, art, and physics, and how these subjects can help them find interesting jobs and careers in 3D technology. The most important goals are to demystify these machines and their abilities, to create an introductory guide with different avenues that allow readers to relate the subject to themselves, and to provide a deeper knowledge of the technology.

Before we dive into the nuts and bolts of additive manufacturing, we will review STEM and STEAM classes that relate directly to learning 3D technology. At this stage, you do not need to know advanced math or be a gifted artist to learn 3D printing. Some of us feel a rising sense of panic at the mention of math or physics; others of us love these subjects but are terrified of painting, for fear of making stick figures.

We are all made differently, and think differently, and as we complete high school we have begun to learn who we are, as part of our lifelong adventure. Part of this is learning how we learn: do we remember lessons better when we can see information as pictures, or is it easier to recall when we have heard the instructor talk? This is the difference between visual and verbal learning.

As an artist, I am a very visual learner. For that reason, I enjoyed diving into CAD programs like Rhino and Tinkercad, and seeing what colorful shapes, forms, and patterns I could produce, with the further excitement of knowing that what I made could likely be sculpted by the printer. I also enjoy the beauty of geometry, and flying around inside the workspace of the software, zooming in and out, and seeing the work from different angles.

Many CAD programs still are a little more designed toward their original audience: engineers, architects, industrial designers, and CAD technicians. A program originally meant for nautical engineers may have a hard time stretching to fit an audience of painters and sculptors. As such, I had to reconcile the left and right sides of my brain, and allow my training in science and technology to help me as an artist to decode what I was looking at, in order to control the programs.

In science, you often have to learn about a new subject area rather quickly, such as surface topography, by reading papers written by scientists. That is where the skill of "reading around the cow" comes into play. Identifying what you do not know can empower you to learn it, and so with CAD, by identifying the subcomponents of how things work, you can master it more easily. See the work of Dr. Richard Feynman, a physicist known as "The Great Explainer!"

This is more easily done if you are mindful of how you learn. Once you are aware of this, you can choose different paths on how you want to learn a subject. In the example of CAD/CAM (computer-assisted manufacturing), you can learn how to make 3D models by manipulating the shapes, or you can learn how to code and program using words and math.

Finally, all of this is done to make a subject easier for you to learn. By learning the tricks of how you learn, how a technology functions, and what the jargon words mean, you can better teach it to yourself, and become an independent learner, tackling new and strange programs. I know this because I have applied these techniques to multiple programs, both for hard science and for artists, as well as beginners. The techniques have been met with success, especially when I have applied the "30,000-foot view" approach. In this chapter you will see how 3D technology can be learned using this simplified approach, also known as a "metacognitive" method.

that is advertised when you see a 3D movie: through optical manipulation, there is added depth to the creature feature.

When you use a desktop printer to print out a copy of the paper you wrote on this book (see what I did there?), you can watch the ink-jet or laser-jet printer head move from left to right to place the letters and words in sequence to create a sentence, in order to reproduce what you typed into the computer. The same thing happened to create this book. The movement of the

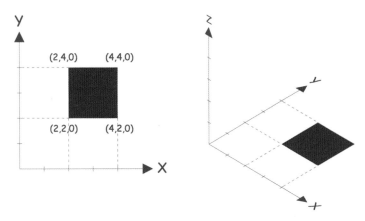

The x, y, and z axes seen here are the foundation for the CAD/CAM creation of an object.

printer head from left to right can be described by the x axis, and the movement of the printer head from the top to the bottom of the page can be described by the y axis. If we add a third dimension, an arrow rising up out of the page, this would be the z axis, and this is exactly how 3D technology works.

For example, in 3D software, such as Rhino, the models are designed using these three axes. This can be achieved by using either the shape tools already included in the program, or by directly entering the coordinates for the different boundaries and points of the object. In 3D printing, such as stereolithography, the addition of layer upon layer of material as a slowly rising stack is performed by telling the printing head of the printer where to move by coordinates in the x, y, and z axes.

This is another good time to consider the origins of STL printing, a modification of resin-coated paper that is

This contact scanner accurately measures the topography of an object to be printed.

printed and stacked. You can start to see now that there are matches between how the software programs are designed and how the printing machines operate. These matches exist because the CAD software has to represent a three-dimensional space that the 3D CAM or printing machines modify.

Input or Acquisition

The first step in creating a 3D model is to create information that the computer can use to produce a 3D print. While this may sound complex, remember that the control of this technology is based on a series of steps. There is a deliberate reason for each of these steps, a choice made by a person acting as a programmer to facilitate the digitization or conversion of the dimensions of an object so that it can be represented and manipulated in a computer program.

When I was studying facial prosthetic treatment, I was fortunate to have an independent study with a very knowledgeable anatomist. He once pointed out that the meaning of the word dissect is "to separate into pieces." In looking at additive manufacturing from the 30,000-foot view, it is helpful to dissect, divide, or separate the process into the components, or steps. The next sections, "The What" and "The How," are focused on dissecting and translating the elements of the processing pipeline.

The What

Let's use some synonyms to make these technical words and ideas work for us. "Input" could also be described as **acquisition**, or the acquiring of information. So, for example, when we scan an object–say, a piece of broken pottery–we are grabbing information in one form by measuring the dimensions of its surface.

Now, thinking of using your laptop or desktop, scanning is not the only way to put information into a computer, right? You can enter information by typing, using a removable hard drive, etc. The most important aspect of inputting information or data into the computer and a given software program is avoiding inaccuracies.

If, for example, you are printing an action figure, you would not want the figure to 3D print with his arm coming out of his head. Unless, of course, that is his superpower. If, on the other hand, you are a doctor or scientist and are 3D printing a bladder, you want as few inaccuracies as possible. To deeply understand this step in the processing pipeline, we should be thinking about what we are going to print and how we are going to do it.

The How

Let's consider three professionals: the artist, the engineer, and the doctor. Each of these people has different needs, expectations, and approaches for their machines, as each is a different person with different training. The artist will want to work more intuitively, that is, without a lot of preplanning, as this can limit the flow of his or her work, which is sometimes the most beautiful aspect. The engineer will want to work methodically and specifically to execute his or her design. The doctor bears the weight of the patient's health. The doctor and engineer will insist on avoiding any inaccuracies.

For each of these professions, there is a way to create input that matches their **workflow**. These methods can include:

- Entering the dimensions manually into the software using x and y coordinates.
- Using a tablet and pen (such as a Wacom tablet) to draw or digitally sculpt the object.
- Scanning the object one of several ways: use a laser/surface or contact scanner, or use a multi-camera setup that takes multiple pictures of an object and stitches them together.

- Importing the file from another program.
- Using a medical tool such as a CT machine to measure the qualities of the patient's anatomy, such as the structure of his or her skull. This can be read in a similar manner as a topographical map.
- The artist, engineer, or doctor also using a combination of these methods to create the result they want.

For now, let's focus on the benefits of each one to the respective individual. The artist enjoys using a sculpting program called ZBrush, which allows him or her to begin with a digital ball of "clay." The artist can then pinch and pull the object into a range of forms, resulting in everything from imaginative character modeling to fine-art statues.

Engineers may prefer a program like Rhino, in which they can precisely control outcomes by entering points to create a line, and then adding more lines to create a 2D shape, like a square. If they then extend this shape up into the z axis, it creates a third dimension, thus making a 3D object. Solidworks is another program that is popular among biomedical engineers, who use it in the creation of customized surgical stents.

The doctor can begin by taking a CT scan of a patient's head, with the keyword being "scan." The "CT" stands for "computed tomography," with "tomos" meaning "slice." This means that during a CT scan, the patient's anatomy is measured in slices, and when it is assembled, these slices are stacked. Are we detecting a theme here?

The CT scan data can then be imported into a 3D CAD program and converted to a digital 3D model, which can then be edited so that the doctor can view different parts of the patient's anatomy. It has been established in craniofacial (skull and face) rehabilitation research (such as for skull fractures) that the cause of most inaccuracies in producing implants for patients using CT data is actually patient movement. The cause is human error and not a computer malfunction.

For each one of these approaches, there is an opportunity for error at the initial input stage. As we established earlier, as of yet, computers are not self-aware or conscious. They can only work with what they are given, and so if they are given bad or erroneous messages by their human users, the computers will produce bad models. This is annoying at best for the artist, and potentially life threatening for the engineer and doctor's clients, such as the driver of a boat or a patient needing a customized implant or medical device.

This is why this first stage of the processing pipeline is the most important, because what goes in must come out. Like a passenger train gathering steam, it is much easier to make changes in direction early on, rather than at the end of the process. And, like a train off the tracks, errors in additive manufacturing can have dramatic consequences.

Pro Concepts: Surface Landmarks

You may say to yourself, "Well, that's all well and good, but didn't you mention laser scanners?" I did! Now that we've covered the general aspects and applications of data input for acquisition in the processing pipeline, we can discuss more complex concepts about scanning.

The reason **landmarks** are relevant to professionals are twofold. First, scans often occur in sections, and then they are put back together, much like how an orange is both whole and sectional. Second, as you'll recall, it takes more and more time and energy to fix errors further and further down the line. Professionals save themselves time, money, and serious consequences from scanning errors by paying careful attention to landmarks.

Matching sectional slices of a scan is one use for landmark surface markers. Another is used in research and industry to match the surfaces of two different objects to one another. If there are two similar features to be measured, such as a particular curve for a skull implant that should match up between the bony surface and the metal, then the CAD model of the curve will be "pinned," or marked, as well as the CAD model of the implant.

Then the two surfaces can be aligned within a particular program, and (this is where it gets interesting) the difference between the two objects can be measured. In everyday terms, the landmarks are used to measure if the skull implant has been made safely enough to fit. This is a form of quality control. In technical language, the landmarks were used for surface difference analysis, and this is of great value in the research areas of areal wavelength science and implantology.

Here is a good way to translate the use of landmarks: Think of taking a road trip. You accidentally take a wrong turn and are now lost. There is no GPS or map app. How do you find your way back? You look for familiar landmarks, such as a donut shop. Similarly, a computer uses landmarks to recognize familiar features of a surface, or two surfaces. If a vase were being laser scanned all the way around, it would be described as being scanned 360 degrees, like a circle.

In order to complete this process, the scanner may have to make multiple scans by scanning sections of the vase at a time. As mentioned before, the approach is similar to how an orange is structured: there are regularly spaced segments, each adding up to a sphere. The scanner will measure landmarks on the surface of the vase, and the software will match similar landmarks together, adding the "slices" together to make the orange. The computer does so by lining up the sections of the slices and stitching the image together.

Processing the What

Speaking of processes, this next step refers to how the computer works with the input information via the software. Some of these steps are automated, and some require feedback from the user, much like driving a car. Ultimately, the human user is in the driver's seat, in control, and responsible for the direction of things.

The largest component of processing that occurs for the artist is what is done by hand within the program. The creative choices that the artist makes to stretch and build an object really center around how the artist distorts the geometry. When he or she is satisfied with the work, the artist will then convert the model to a printable file type.

An engineer is working with an emphasis on precision. The artist may adapt to or even enjoy unexpected things happening within the making process, but it is essential that things are predictable for the engineer. As a result, the programs, like Rhino, that engineers use are logically built around math and geometry, both of which have clear and simple rules.

A surgeon may want a customized model of a skull in order to explain to the patient what he or she is experiencing and to educate the patient on his or her options. The surgeon may also use the model of the skull for practicing different surgical options without the pressure and seriousness of having a live patient on the operating table. In order to print the skull, the surgeon, **anaplastologist,** maxillofacial prosthetist, or prosthodontist would take the CT scan data, import it into the appropriate software, delete the extraneous anatomy that they do not want represented (this can

GODFREY HOUNSFIELD

Godfrey Hounsfield was awarded the Nobel Prize in Physiology or Medicine in 1979, but he spent a lifetime at the forefront of the technical revolution of the twentieth century. He credited his upbringing on a farm in Nottinghamshire, England, where he had hours of alone time to experiment away from the distractions of the city.

As he wrote in an autobiographical sketch after receiving the Nobel Prize, "I made hazardous investigations of the principles of flight, launching myself from the tops of haystacks with a home-made glider; I almost blew myself up during exciting experiments using water-filled tar barrels and acetylene to see how high they could be waterjet propelled. It may now be a trick of the memory but I am sure that on one occasion I managed to get one to an altitude of 1,000 feet [305 m]!"

This curiosity helped him get recognized during World War II, during which he worked on radar and radio communications. This earned him a grant to attend college, after which he worked on the development of the computer. He led the design team that built the first all-transistor computer in Britain. Following the failure of one of his research projects, he came up with the idea that greatly influenced medicine.

"One of the suggestions I put forward was connected with automatic pattern recognition and it was while exploring various aspects of pattern recognition and their potential, in 1967, that the idea occurred to me which was eventually to become the EMI-Scanner and the technique of computed tomography," he wrote.

Hounsfield developed a unit to measure how easily a material can be penetrated by a beam of light, sound, particles, or other energy or matter. Uses include measuring the fat content of a liver or bone mineral density.

The lifelong bachelor dedicated his life to his work, which included advances in CT technology and diagnostic imaging. He died in 2004.

be done by changing the Hounsfield value, or level of radiodensity, which is the property of obstructing the passage of radiant energy such as X-rays), and save the file once it is reduced to the skull only.

Another way to think of this step is zooming in or out of the different layers of tissue within the head to get to the part of interest—e.g., bone. As anyone who has merely looked at an anatomy textbook can confirm, there is a lot of stuff and parts in the human head (medically speaking). As a result, tools that help navigate all of the physical complexity of the head and neck are helpful to both the patient and the care provider. The area of anatomy can also be selected or cropped, such as the orbit. This edited and prepared model can then be sent to the printer for production.

Processing the How

For the engineer working within Rhino, it is important to be mindful of how his or her model is built to help with any troubleshooting in the future. The cube the engineer has built is actually a combination of surfaces. Remember how the cube was built from points to lines to a square?

That square would actually be considered a plane, and this plane with four corners and four parallel lines would become a cube, itself consisting of six planes. The planes would then be combined to form a solid: instead of separate parts that look like a single object, the cube is now one object.

As we saw earlier, the doctor working to create an anatomical model is using CT information. Remember that a CT scan works in sections, allowing it to be matched with the stereolithography model that is to be built layer by layer. These slices can be used to create 3D pixels, or voxels. A voxel is a unit of graphical information that defines a point in three-dimensional space (this is another example of the use of the x, y, and z axes).

The voxels are then converted via computer programming to a file type called DICOM. The DICOM data is then sent to a 3D program such as Mimics by Materialise. The DICOM file is then converted to a CAD file type that can be edited by the user. In the prior example of the model of the skull, the file can be edited to create custom guides for implants as well.

It should be noted that the purpose of programs such as Mimics is to act as facilitator. In other words, the program makes a difficult job easier, while still maintaining a high standard of safety and avoiding inaccuracy. By creating schematic representations with animated tool and editing features, programs like this allow medical specialists to increase the pace and reduce the inaccuracy of treatment.

This next step is an important one to understanding how the CAD design is prepared to print. When, for example, a model of an engine part is being made within a software program, the CAD file often has a named file type that is based on the program it is in—e.g., Rhino or Solidworks. That proprietary file type is sent to the printer, but it may require preformatting. Behold, the entry of the mighty STL file extension. The CAD file needs to be converted into what is called an "STL file," or a file with a name that ends with ".stl."

Designed for stereolithography, STL can also represent "standard triangulation language." Imagine the 3D model of a gear, floating happily on a computer screen. Now, try to imagine the gear as though it is made out of wire mesh. It's easy to see that the pattern of this mesh is made of tiled or repeating shapes, and in the case of CAD, the mesh is made of triangles. This file is now in the correct format to be "read" or understood by a 3D printer. However, this is also the point where the greatest inaccuracies can occur.

That is because there are many, many, many triangles involved in producing an STL file, involving many calculations by the computer, and as a result, there are many opportunities for errors. These errors are represented as "holes" in the wire mesh and are referred to as "naked edges." These holes can throw off the printer, leading to errors or simply resulting in an inability to print.

The model must therefore be prepared to be sent to the printer by being without any open holes or naked edges. The command in Rhino is to "Fill All Holes," and when this is successfully completed, the model can be sent to the 3D printer without problems. The model is then considered "watertight," the goal of processing before 3D printing.

It can be helpful when learning a subject to be provided with concrete examples. In this spirit, let's consider the software program Rhino. To summarize the ground-up construction of a 3D model within Rhino, the model is built using geometry by starting with a point, adding points to create lines, adding lines to create a plane, adding planes to create a multi-surface object (such as a cube), the unification of planes to make a solid, and the conversion of a CAD file into a "watertight" polygon mesh to be sent to the printer.

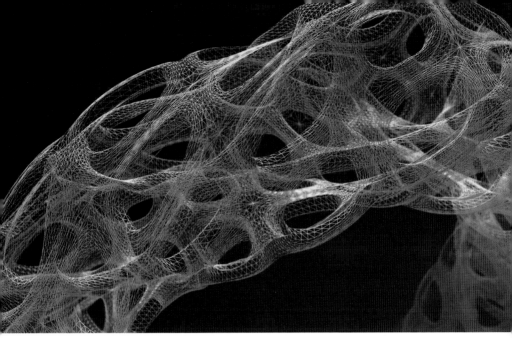

This image has been produced in a software program, and it looks like wire mesh (think of the screen doors and windows in your home). The reason it looks like wire mesh is that this model consists of many triangles that have been arranged together in a tiled pattern.

All of these steps would be considered processing after the initial acquisition, the purpose of which is to make the data more compressed and usable to the programs that will allow it to be modeled. In other words, the processing step is essential in converting the acquired information into a more usable format. The purpose of the use may be varied but ultimately based around 3D printing, or output.

Output

This step refers to the actual physical manufacturing of the 3D-printed object. As discussed earlier, the digital file sent to the printer must be as "clean" as possible. As you'll recall from chapter 2, there are many printing methods and materials to choose from. The following examples of our professionals at work are just a brief selection of what is possible.

The artist has decided to print a sculpture using an online 3D printing business. With this method, the artist (as the client) simply has to upload a file through the 3D printing business's website. Once the file is uploaded, the company may contact the artist with any file issues (such as naked edges). It may also contact the artist if there are any design questions, such as a preferred color, material, or finish. In this case, the artist decided to create his or her sculptural vision using SLS plastic for a contemporary look.

The engineer's challenge has been to produce a customized prototype for a plane. The engineer has chosen to produce a custom titanium plane strut, using titanium powder. Remember, as the part has been made from powder, there is the risk that there are imperfections or even holes within the solid part that are not visible to the naked eye. The part can be checked for inaccuracies or material failures using a CT scanner.

Our surgeon will print the patient's skull by coordinating with the craniofacial team within the hospital. They will use a stereolithography printer on an in-house machine. By having the technology and properly trained professionals on staff, the hospital can save time and money as well as increase coordination between the doctor and 3D printing specialist. This is of value if the doctor wants to focus on a specific area of the skull or if there are any inaccuracies present. In other words, it gives the medical staff more control over the tools that they use to ensure a high quality of medical care, while opening the possibilities for new treatment and research.

Finishing

If up to this point we have been thinking of the 3D print as a cake that is being prepared, baked, and taken out of the oven, then finishing is the step when we have completed the hard work and get to have fun. This is the moment we can add the icing and marzipan flowers! In other words, we are literally finishing the process, and this step applies to any post-printing or postproduction treatments or procedures that are done to the object or material.

For the artist, this could mean adding paint or sealant to the sculpture to change its color or texture. For the engineer, it can mean removing any supports or artifacts from the printing process, such as by waterjet or grinding. For the doctor, this can mean sandblasting a custom titanium implant to improve the implant's chance of success within the body. All of these are done to improve the usefulness of the print, and to maximize the effectiveness of the 3D print for its end use, such as display or sale in a gallery, supporting the structural integrity of an aircraft, or improving surgical outcomes and patient safety.

TECHNICAL TERMS

medical illustration A visual translation of complex medical or biological information to be used in patient education and medical research.

ocularist A person who makes and fits artificial eyes.

stereophotogrammetry The process of making a 3D model based on the positions of recognizable points or landmarks in several different photographs.

CHAPTER FOUR

Union of Art and Science

T
HERE IS AN EVER-INCREASING NUMBER OF FIELDS AND JOBS that are embracing or require knowledge of how to use 3D technology. This includes knowledge of the theory behind the technology and an ability to use it creatively, as well as jobs that need a concrete technical or technological understanding of how to operate the machines. By pursuing your passions, you can unlock new areas of interest that you may not have been aware of previously.

My parents always told me: "Do what you love and the money will follow." In other words, if you can enfold your passions into your career, this will allow you to pursue

Opposite: The reproduction of the Palmyra Arch of Triumph in Trafalgar Square shows a creative way to retain a cultural legacy.

your dreams. You will be amazed at how much energy, drive, and focus is possible as a result.

In high school, one of my favorite things to do was to go to a local coffee shop, buy a ginger soda, and then walk down the block to the local bookstore, Talking Leaves. I loved the smell of the freshly published books and the sheer volume of information contained there, all the possibilities of knowledge, experiences, and travel. It was there that I found the book *The Diving Bell and the Butterfly*, by Jean-Dominique Bauby.

Bauby was the French editor of *Elle* magazine and a family man before suffering a massive stroke that left him able to move only his left eyelid but completely coherent mentally. This condition is known as locked-in syndrome, and eventually Bauby learned to communicate by blinking. He then wrote an entire memoir by blinking each letter so that it could be written down. He passed away two days after the book was published.

The power and humanity of the book resonated with me in how our internal worlds remain while we struggle with changes to our bodies. It also struck me artistically, as I had developed a passion for drawing and painting portraits of friends and family, and even from magazines. Pretty much anything I could get my hands on that made for an interesting portrait, I painted. Faces fascinated me, and I poured over books on drawing anatomy, especially the works of Burne Hogarth, and later the Old Masters, such as Leonardo da Vinci. I repeatedly copied the masters' drawings as well as I could, trying to learn the nuances of our features.

Science was also a great interest of mine, especially human evolution. I was fascinated with how our ancestors' faces changed over time, first with diet, then speech, and then the influence of technology. As high school drew to a close, I was having trouble deciding what to study in college. A friend suggested **medical illustration** because I would be able to incorporate both art and science.

I was fortunate to receive a BFA in medical illustration during an interesting time: the transition in the field from primarily traditional techniques like graphite and carbon dust to digital programs like Adobe Photoshop and Illustrator. People were also diving into 3D programs like Rhino and 3D Studio Max/Maya, and producing biological animations. I also felt particularly lucky to be mentored in studio and conceptual art at a time when my mind was also being expanded by the concepts I was learning in my science classes, especially human embryology.

A career-changing moment came when I won an internship with a medical illustrator who had changed his own career path and become an **ocularist,** Frederic Harwin. An ocularist is a clinician who treats patients missing one or both eyes by providing custom-made prosthetic eyes. Each prosthesis is hand-made, including a painted iris. The prothetic eye supports the shape of the lid, helps the orbital mucles keep their tone, protects sensitive tissue inside the eyelid, and gives the wearer the appearance of binocular vision. After seeing the difference in the quality of life that a patient experiences upon receiving a new artificial eye, I was hooked on prosthetic treatment.

ART
RESTORATION

Beyond the human lives lost during the rise of ISIS (Islamic State in Iraq and Syria) has been the loss of items from antiquity. Buildings and artworks that have survived for millennia have been destroyed by members of this group.

However, 3D technology and printing have helped bring some of these lost items back to life. Artist Morehshin Allahyari has worked with other artists and cultural groups to create 3D-printable copies of work thought to have been destroyed in Iraq's Mosul Museum. The pieces are available for downloading and printing so anyone can make a copy of these historic items.

Digital imaging is also helping to restore architecture destroyed by ISIS. The Institute of Digital Archaeology used images of Palmyra's Arch of Triumph, destroyed during ISIS's occupation of the ancient city, to build a scale model of the arch for display in London's Trafalgar Square. Photographs of the original arch, which was built by the Romans, were used to make 3D images of the arch that could be entered into design software. The software guided milling equipment that carved the two-thirds scale model out of marble to appear as the arch did at the time of its destruction—an example of computer-aided manufacturing (CAM).

"We can never have the same image as before ISIS," said Maamoun Abdulkarim, Syria's director of antiquities. "We are trying to be realistic. But what we want to do is respect the scientific method and the identity of Palmyra as a historic site."

Scanning and 3D printing can help to archive and reproduce ancient art, such as this Assyrian sculpture in Iraq.

I am now proud to say that one of my professions is fine art, and the second is in science and medicine as an anaplastologist. I am fortunate to provide prosthetic treatment to patients who have lost parts of their face to cancer or trauma, or were born without them. This includes eyes, ears, noses, larger parts of the eye anatomy (called the orbit), and even larger parts of the face. My role is both clinical and technological, and so I must act as both information and manual worker to ensure the best possible care.

These patients need extra care in several areas. First, because they are often affected psychologically by their condition, they may need someone who can be an active listener, as they are usually deeply processing a trauma and grief for the loss of an important part of themselves. Everyone knows what their ear looks like, and feels attached because it is theirs, and no one else's. The sudden loss of it can be very overwhelming, especially when it is coupled with the news of a serious illness.

Second, the patients need prostheses to help restore their appearance. The prosthetics care provider can come from several different backgrounds but ultimately needs to have training and education that is appropriate to clinical treatment as well as an ability to produce lifelike prostheses. In my case, I began my training in medical illustration and ocularistry, then anaplastology and medical sculpture at Johns Hopkins School of Medicine with Juan Garcia, and then craniofacial prosthetics, implants, and technology.

I was exposed to 3D printing technology during my training in anaplastology and medical sculpture for both clinical and research purposes. During my training, I was fortunate to see how patients with facial trauma or differences were benefiting from the creative and informed use of scanning and additive manufacturing. The use of surface scanning and stereolithography impressed me immediately as I saw it being used to improve patient safety for implant guidance procedures. The hospital and surgical setting quickly conveyed the seriousness of both the need for and use of the technology.

I later saw even more possibilities of 3D technology for quality control as I pursued my master's degree in maxillofacial and craniofacial technology. The degree from King's College London focused on the role of being involved in both the clinic and in research, known as a clinical researcher. The clinical focus was on patient safety via a knowledgeable and well-trained clinician, and excellence in research via exposure to a breadth of digital and biomaterial technologies.

This included **stereophotogrammetry**, **spectrophotometry**, 3D CAD programs for anatomical modeling, contact surface scanning, and exposure to a number of other technologies, including powder bed fusion. The applications largely involved quality control for facial prosthetic and surgical rehabilitation, such as: anatomical modeling for patient education; custom surgical guides for implant placement; custom craniofacial implants, such as for cheekbone augmentation for birth conditions; customized titanium skull and eye-socket repair implants; and measurement of the fit of custom implants.

After exposure to all of these medical benefits of 3D technology, I moved back to the United States just as the home market for 3D printing took off like a rocket. I was hired to teach college courses in 3D printing, designing curriculum for both art and science, and eventually leading faculty training sessions and helping to secure grants for a 3D printing center. Simultaneously I began being hired for lectures on translating the often technical language of 3D technologies to general audiences, as there was a sudden surge of interest in the public about the innovative technology and its applications.

I also became a resident artist, and received sponsorship from 3Doodler™ for a series of installations, beginning my passionate interest in the use of 3D printing pens in fine-arts applications. As I mentioned earlier, this emerging technology allows me to translate my process from traditional 2D creation into 3D sculptural forms. Being involved in a variety of 3D technologies during this crossover period, in which many of the emerging technologies described earlier are now becoming sustaining and mainstream, is exhilarating.

We have explored how 3D printing is what we call a gateway technology because it allows for new technologies to emerge as it flourishes. As a result, 3D printing can also be seen as a technology that unlocks new career possibilities. It opens up new career fields, cross-collaboration, and even the blending of professional disciplines (known as interdisciplinary). I can vouch for this based on my personal and professional experience as an artist, scientist, and clinician, and I have also included an interview with my friend who is an engineer, designer, and maker in the following pages.

This technological crossover ability can be seen in the way things are made (design, manufacturing, and invention) and also how 3D printing can be used as a tool to do other activities, such as research. The following paragraphs are a survey of and introduction to different professions that use or are involved with 3D printing. As you read the pages ahead, keep in mind what is fun for you and what you love to do, and how 3D printing can help you find a profession, or create one, that incorporates your passions and goals.

Engineering

Centuries ago, the standardization of parts permitted the Industrial Revolution, in that objects and parts could be made quickly and repeatedly by being of the same dimensions. It became important to illustrate how these parts were and are made clearly and with as few inaccuracies as possible. Mechanical drawing refers to how drawings and plans are produced for parts for industrial production. Examples of these parts include boat motors, car axles, and airplane elements such as struts.

AN INTERVIEW WITH ERIK VOELKLE

Erik Voelkle of Viking Design Works in Buffalo, New York, is a 3D printing designer, engineer, and maker. Here he replies to five questions about his career.

Q: What do you like the most about being a 3D technology engineer, designer, and maker?

A: I think what I love most about 3D technology and design/making is the ability to be more creative than we have been in the past. In additive manufacturing, we can get away with design techniques that were not available or were extremely difficult and costly in traditional machining. I also love the fact that I can come up with an idea and have it in my hands in a few short hours. That is just too cool.

Q: What are some of the most interesting projects that you have worked on?

A: I would have to say my most interesting project to date was designing a three-gear transmission case for a specific remote-controlled buggy. I spent two weeks of all my free time engulfed in reverse-engineering and designing at the same time, and I loved every minute of the project. Also, a differential service station tool; I wanted it to look aesthetically pleasing, yet be highly functional. It has been my best seller to date.

Q: What schooling best prepared you for your career in 3D technology?

A: Honestly, for me it was the opportunity to learn 3D modeling hands on. I am not one that typically does well with textbooks or charts. I found that I learned the basics quite quickly by just playing around with the software and doing a few online tutorials. I think maybe it was important to learn the basics of 2D first. That helped too.

Q: Based on that, what do you feel are the most important skills for students to have who want to go into 3D technology and printing?

A: Based on that, I would have to say the most important skills to have for students would be to practice being able to visualize 2D projections. From that, you can shape and form the best way in 3D to achieve your design and printing goals. The more practice you can have visualizing your end result, and how to get to that point via technology, the better. It will help you streamline your design process.

Q: What excites you most about the future of 3D technology?

A: I think what excites me most about the future of 3D technology is we are just on the cusp of 3D printing being a huge disrupting force in society. As 3D technology becomes more and more accessible to everyone, the creativity and ability to design, make, and use items in our life will change significantly. I only see 3D technology getting bigger and bigger, and its uses spreading wider and wider.

Some of the largest and most well-known 3D modeling programs were initially created for mechanical drawing and rendering. As we learned in earlier chapters, the logic for these programs is shared because they were developed using the language and vocabulary of engineers, and they were designed to make sure these parts are made well and with reliable accuracy. These programs build 3D models by beginning with 2D geometry. If you are interested in a career that allows you to design or help create exciting machines like submarines, helicopters, and race cars, one of the most important skills you can learn is how to do basic drawing, and how that translates to the computer environment.

Art: Visualization and Rehabilitation

The power of art lies in the ability to make the unknown visible, to bring the intangible from the imagination into the real world. Tools that facilitate this visualization can be highly useful to artists. 3D printing helps artists produce work that would either be impossible to produce in other ways, such as highly complex geometric shapes, or that would take a very long time to produce by hand.

In my own artwork, I use the 3Doodler pen to produce three-dimensional single-line drawings. This technology allows me to have an intuitive interaction with the manufacturing component of the 3D printing technology: the printer head. I do not have to preplan what I want to create in software, or scan in one of my

Gateway technologies free artists to fabricate and print freehand. Seen here is one of the author's installations from 2016.

drawings to be processed in software and then sent to the printer. I can change what I want to create as I go, and that is exactly how my pen-and-ink drawings are produced.

In other words, I can directly transfer my art process (or how an artist develops and produces art) from 2D to 3D without much difference. This is very appealing to artists as they can "stay in the zone" without breaking concentration, and this allows them to make better art.

3D printing also allows artists to work when they might not be able to otherwise. Consider sculpting done by hand: hundreds if not thousands of hours spent standing, chiseling, and molding stone, clay, or wax into statues, installations, or even mobiles. This exhilarating endeavor can come at a price, however: this physical work can take its toll on the body over time, limiting what older artists, or those with illness or injury, can achieve.

In her book 3D *Technology in Fine Art and Craft*, artist and author Bridgette Mongeon describes how 3D software and printing allowed her to return to her art after she experienced severe pain while working. By using ZBrush and 3D printing, Mongeon could make sculptures again. Without the invention and development of 3D technology into a format that artists could use, Mongeon, along with many other older artists, would have to face some difficult choices.

3D technologies can also help in art preservation and restoration. A very famous example of art that has been reproduced via laser scanning and printing frequently is the statue *David* by Michelangelo. The scanning of such works is a scientifically vetted method of preserving the features and conditions of the work in archival form. A benefit to the creation of a digital model is that it can also be shared and reproduced globally, as well as make some pretty classy refrigerator magnets.

Business and Innovation

The United States was founded with the goal of creating a republic free from the restrictions and tyranny of a monarch, or king. This freedom from rule also meant freedom from any sort of caste system. That is why we do not have nobility in the United States. This desire for social freedom and movement was coupled with a thirst for economic freedom as well.

We also wanted to be free to make money: New York City, "New Amsterdam," was founded by the Dutch as a trading post. This is why we have two capitals, one for government and one for business—Washington, DC, and New York City—whereas most other nations have only one, e.g., London or Paris. Fueled by these dual drives of free thinking and financial aspirations, the country developed a thirst for innovation.

Think of some of the most famous names in invention and business of the last two centuries: Nikola Tesla, Madam C. J. Walker, George Washington Carver, Thomas Edison, Hedy Lamarr, George R. Carruthers, Buckminster Fuller. Even Abraham Lincoln held a patent! Invention is seen as the gateway to wealth and prosperity. With innovation comes patents and intellectual property; with intellectual property comes revenue!

The value that 3D printing and technologies provide can best be seen in the use of software programs like Rhino and Solidworks. Companies like Nike, New Balance, and Boeing regularly use these programs to develop and 3D print prototypes for new products, from new running shoes to plane parts. 3D printing provides an opportunity to rapidly produce new concepts and, in a competitive global marketplace, make changes. This last component cannot be overemphasized in terms of value. Whether adapting to new fashion trends (such as bright neon colors) or important structural changes (so that planes do not break down midair), the ability to quickly produce

New Balance made these shoes with a multimaterial printer. Such tools are indispensable for companies in competitive marketplaces.

and make changes to concept and marketing models is of great value to companies.

Thinking back to the invention of stereolithography, when Charles Hull presented his machines to the boards of companies, the businesspersons initially had a hard time understanding their value, let alone how they worked. Now printers such as the ones capable of multimaterial printing are seen as indispensable tools.

Innovation, Entrepreneurship, and Making

A desire for independence is as central to the American spirit as the genius for invention and a yearning for economic mobility. This is as true among the punk rockers of NYC as it is among the Amish of Pennsylvania

Dutch country. An emblem of this part of our nature is our DIY culture, which can be seen at home, in our renewed appreciation for fixer-uppers; in the roadsters on our streets; and perhaps most of all, in maker culture.

Ask your grandparents or great-grandparents, and they will tell you that during the twentieth century, when you bought a stereo, a coffee maker, or especially a car, it was expected that you could repair it, or learn how to repair it, yourself. If you needed help, you could turn to publications like *Popular Mechanics* and get step-by-step instructions. This provided a sense of independence, both in terms of self-reliance through learning and economic control.

Once purchased, a big investment could be maintained for years or decades. (If you ever hear them complaining about everything being made cheaply these days, this is why!) Many people who experienced the Great Depression as children, or those who received the habits gained by their parents during that time, understood that sometimes you had to repair instead of buy new. Sometimes, you could not afford a repairman or mechanic, and had to do it yourself.

In the past half century, the United States and Canada as part of a global community have experienced a cultural jolt as technology- and information-based jobs have bypassed those requiring manual skill. This has coincided with the emergence of the home computer, the internet, cell and smartphones, social media, and, of course, 3D technology. There is, however, a continuous line of self-reliance between the pioneer homesteaders who had to fix their own tools and the rise of RepRap.

Makers identify with the creative and often artistic crossover between analog tools and technology, such as woodworking and metalworking (even blacksmithing), and the digital universe, including circuit kits (like Arduino and Raspberry Pi) and 3D technology ranging from printers to subtractive manufacturing devices like CNC machines. There is a focus on sharing, including in learning, and classes are regularly held at meet-ups and makerspaces. These are held at DIY spaces with room and the durability for plenty of people, tools, saws, gears, computers, printers, electronics, robots, noise, and fun.

Most of the projects that makers like to engage with and share are decidedly DIY and low-cost. They often modify existing machines or technology. This is because there is also a crossover with hacker culture and computer culture, where there are always new updates, memes, and ideas. The focus is on community and open sharing, and the ideas and techniques of modifying technology provide a sense of independence and control over it. You can see why RepRap printers that are open source and can print their own replacement parts would be a natural fit and hit with a community like this.

Maker Faires, where talented makers can showcase their ideas and attendees can pick up new techniques, are becoming more and more common in cities throughout the United States. DIY makerspaces and Fab Labs are also hotbeds of innovation. Once people learn how to modify the technology, their natural creativity opens up new possibilities. This pattern has repeated itself to the extent that it has caught the attention of the federal government. In 2014, President Barack Obama offered to open several national research centers to the public. Walk into public libraries in cities around the country, and there is often a space designated for learning new digital skills, such as 3D printing. Making fever has hit!

Fab Labs and makerspaces are a great place to receive a free or low-cost introduction to 3D technology. It's been my experience that people who like to make usually are very welcoming, in part because they want to share the cool stuff that they came up with, and also because they want to learn what you know as well. And learning how to print on inexpensive hardware can always lead to working on the big, expensive, industrial-scale printers.

How can you find out more about making and makerspaces near you? A great resource is *Make* magazine, which provides a forum for the maker community as well as featured projects. The publication naturally caught my eye after seeing a cover story on how to build a DIY robotic hand prosthesis.

Maker culture is the public face of our hunger for innovation and continues to spur low-cost opportunities for new approaches to a wide range of applications for both industry and home use, ranging from robotics to home automation. Our increasing public familiarity and subsequent skill with digital technology and especially

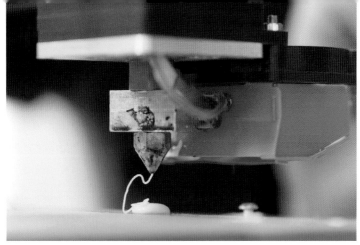

FDM or FFF printers are omnipresent at makerspaces due to the printers' relative low cost and reliability.

3D printing is accelerating our ability to control our home devices and is contributing to our everyday independence.

The Big Picture

Nationally and globally, governments are investing billions of dollars into the development of 3D technologies, as well as into business start-ups that incorporate them. A start-up is a new business, often with a new business model and a product or service that has not been available previously. Many cities, especially in the Great Lakes region, are transitioning from twentieth-century industrial production, such as steel and cars, to twenty-first-century technology, focusing on medical and information technology. 3D modeling and imaging is a natural fit for these new goals.

There are several ways that you can become involved in this movement toward advanced digital and biotechnology. You can get training that will help you succeed as an employee, an employer, or an inventor and maker who creates things that can be sold or used for profit. To become an employee, you want to have skills that are valuable to someone who runs or is starting a business that uses these skills. In other words, to get a job at a 3D printing company, you want to be able to use 3D technology to produce things.

The opportunities that are available require receiving training as a technician or specialist in CAD or CAM. There are a range of levels of training and degrees for these roles, from two-year associate certificates to masters' degrees. There are more jobs in CAD right now than qualified candidates because not enough people are pursuing training (think back to the discussions about STEM and STEAM initiatives).

There are several pathways to becoming an employer. One is to get a business degree. You are then seen as professionally attractive to a company, increasing the likelihood that you can join a business and get promoted from within. You can also start your own company, either by yourself as a sole proprietorship or with other people as a partnership.

Once you have a company, a business idea, and (ideally) a business plan, you can even attract what are called "angel investors," or just regular investors. These are people that want to give money to you and your business with the agreement that it will be used for your business. They often expect a share of the profits or even partial ownership of your company in return. In dollars, this translates to trading more money in your pocket for less stress at the time of startup, plus the chance to make more money overall, such as by having more sales staff.

The reason so much energy, money, and attention is paid to fueling the emergence of new businesses is that the health of the US economy is based on growth. New businesses equal new jobs and new economic growth. 3D modeling and printing assist in the creation of new businesses by making new types of products, parts, and inventions, as well as by allowing the reproduction of old parts.

Remember, new inventions mean new intellectual property. New businesses spring from new inventions. Remember also that 3D technology is a gateway technology, with new technologies emerging from it. 3D technology permits new business growth on multiple levels, with new products, new technologies, and even new gateway technologies, such as self-assembling printing, or 4D printing.

Universities, Laboratories, and Research

The term "4D printing" is used by the Self-Assembly Lab at Massachusetts Institute of Technology. Skylar Tibbits drew a lot of attention to this new approach to additive manufacturing after a TED talk in which he described the future applications of the tech for a variety of fields. This includes a range of industrial needs, from self-assembling furniture to space exploration. The strength of these innovations is rooted in both the material and geometric design of the MIT team's prototypes.

Skylar Tibbits and the MIT Self-Assembly Lab are pioneering the field of 4D printing, or self-assembling objects and patterns.

Large corporations and universities have cultivated research, hiring, and commerce relationships for decades. The concentration of intelligent minds, facilities, and opportunities for new business development makes universities fertile grounds for cultivating business incubation as well as intellectual property.

Cities like New York, Boston, Washington, DC, Chicago, and San Francisco are well-known for their university-hospital-research complexes that fuel both intellectual capital and economic growth. Smaller cities like Buffalo, New York; Portland, Oregon; and Austin, Texas, have also utilized this economic model successfully. This approach is synergistic with the support of innovation centers, coworking spaces, and Fab Labs. Vader Systems was produced as a result of a collaboration with the University at Buffalo Engineering

Department, which allowed the Vaders and their employees to explore their concept in an environment that offered the needed equipment, people, and space.

Aerospace and Architecture

In addition to the previously described applications of AM for airplane design, manufacturing, and repair, there are also future applications. Contour Crafting and Foster and Partners have submitted designs and proposals for utilizing the soil, or regolith—areas of rock sitting on top of unconsolidated bedrock—of the moon and on Mars to produce custom-made, 3D-printed buildings such as space stations. Contour Crafting is developing the technology to 3D print buildings made of concrete, using extruding technology.

MIT is also printing concrete, and NASA has produced a specialized form of AM called electron beam freeform fabrication (EBF3) for customized metal parts. It has also focused on the development of 3D printing food, such as pizza, in space. Astronauts would be able to enjoy freshly made pizza, instead of one that has been preserved or freeze-dried for storage.

The companies mentioned earlier are part of a growing group of firms that are keen to demonstrate their ability to rapidly print a home or complex building. The first question you may ask yourself is "Why? Why attempt to 3D print a building?" Well, the first answer, of course, is, "Why not?" As a species, we generally do not shy away from challenges. There are more specific answers, however.

There are several reasons that this area of architecture is experiencing rapid growth and attention. All too frequently, there is an environmental or weather disaster, war, or epidemic that suddenly creates a need for many shelters very quickly so that the affected people may be protected and cared for. 3D printing of simple concrete shelters offers the opportunity for durable housing that can be produced to meet the needs arising from emergency situations.

Another advantage to automated construction is that it eliminates a great deal of material waste, including the packing for the construction materials, human error, and environmental effects, such as pollution and the carbon footprint. There is also the human factor, such as how construction in some parts of the world is sometimes subject to government corruption. The use of technology may reduce the risk of this type of drawback by simplifying the processes involved in building.

Finally, as mentioned earlier, there are the future goals of interplanetary architecture! There are already plans to use the powder-like lunar dust (regolith) as the build medium for large-scale 3D printing on the moon. The advantage of doing so would be the same as the example of tools described previously. Flight payload is reduced, as well as fuel, and the logistics are simplified. This approach could also work on Mars, which is also dusty like the moon and, as far as we know, lacks natural resources for more traditional building techniques. There will be no log cabins built on Mars.

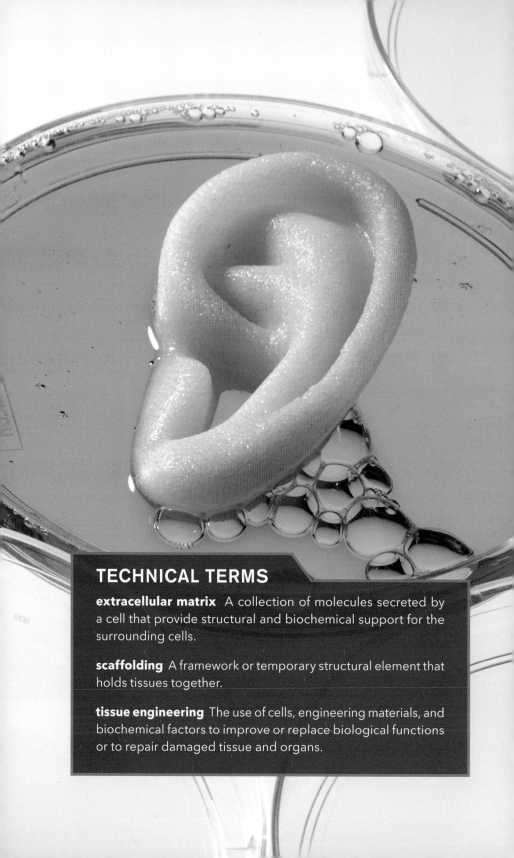

TECHNICAL TERMS

extracellular matrix A collection of molecules secreted by a cell that provide structural and biochemical support for the surrounding cells.

scaffolding A framework or temporary structural element that holds tissues together.

tissue engineering The use of cells, engineering materials, and biochemical factors to improve or replace biological functions or to repair damaged tissue and organs.

CHAPTER FIVE

Medicine and Academics

A S PREVIOUSLY MENTIONED, MY COLLEGE DEGREE WAS IN medical illustration. During my college days, the sentence that truly rocked my world was, "A cell is the fundamental unit of life." This statement by my professor in his slight Texas accent highlighted how within our bodies live trillions of individual cells that collectively form us! How do all of these tiny things stay organized enough to form heads, arms, and legs that can play the piano, pilot a space shuttle, or bust out sweet dance moves?

The answer lies in tissue **scaffolding** known as the **extracellular matrix**. Think of big cities like New York or

Opposite: Organ printing is now a reality, but the long-term success of complex structures like ears continues to challenge researchers.

Los Angeles. They have signature skyscrapers that define their skyline. The support system for these buildings is geometric grids known as scaffolding. Now, within these buildings dwell people, their pets, and houseplants. All of these diverse living beings exist and move about within rooms and halls that are supported within a 3D grid, or matrix.

When our cells are inside our bodies, they are generally within tissues, and when the cells dwell in the tissues, the cells exist within extracellular matrices, or ECM. They live within 3D grids. Remembering our old friends the x, y, and z axes, we can easily describe a grid using math vocabulary, whether huge and towering like the Empire State Building, or microscopic and dynamic like the flexible organizational structure of our bladders.

Remember also the analogy of the desktop printer and a 3D printer? **Tissue engineering** and organ printing got their start when an empty ink-jet cartridge was filled with collagen and connected to a desktop printer. Collagen could then be printed in a regular structure, a macro version of how our tissues are structured microscopically. In other words, the concepts of x, y, and z axes were combined with medical knowledge and an understanding of how our bodies work. See? All that algebra and biology was worth it!

The combination of biological material and mechanical parts would be an example of an application of the principles of 3D printing to create a new technology and a new field: organ printing. This is an

The ear, tissue engineered on the mouse, may not survive when transplanted if there is not a proper blood supply.

example of a gateway technology creating another gateway technology, an event that is rare over the course of human history and that is happening now with increasing frequency due to the invention of more and more gateway technologies.

Just look at the image of the mouse with an ear on its back. The human ear that lived on the mouse's back was grown, not transplanted there. This is important to note as one of the ongoing challenges for medicine and tissue engineering is the longevity of the organ and tissue transplants. This challenge is only increased by the long list of people who need organs replaced.

One core problem is the difficulty in sending blood supply and nutrients to the transplanted organ, such as an ear. The ear may be beautifully formed, but if there are not enough blood vessels, such as arteries, veins, and capillaries, connected to the tissue, then the tissue will not survive. It is the same approach as repotting a plant without roots: without roots, the plant cannot obtain the sustenance it needs to survive.

This is why there has been a focus lately on developing reliable methods of incorporating channels into 3D-printed tissues. The artificial tissues are more likely to survive as a result of designing the artificial blood vessels into the tissues. An example of this is the work that is ongoing at Wake Forest University, led by Dr. Anthony Atala using the Integrated Tissue and Organ Printing System (ITOP).

Dr. Atala was convinced of the need for better treatment options after seeing many patients suffer and pass away because they did not have any options for organ replacement. He decided to commit himself to research that would lead to a genuine solution to the organ donor problem. Dr. Atala felt that this solution lay in 3D printing.

His team's efforts at the Wake Forest Institute for Regenerative Medicine (WFIRM) have resulted in a true 3D organ printer. Unlike previous machines that produce a matrix that still has to be prepared by being infused with living cells, the ITOP merges those actions in one machine. The value of this is that it prints living biological tissue.

Dr. Anthony Atala at Wake Forest University works with a bladder created with the help of additive manufacturing.

The value of Dr. Atala and his colleagues' work is that an artificial organ that has been populated by a patient's own cells would share the patient's DNA. The artificial organ transplant would not be recognized as a foreign body that would lead to an immune response and possibly rejection. On the human side of things, this research also would spare a lot of heartache. It would prevent patients from needing a donor; this current reality means that for some organs, the original donor must have passed away. The grim math of this would no longer be needed with custom-made organs.

There are other areas of research at WFIRM, including direct tissue printing for wound repair, stem cell repair, printing skin for burns patients, artificial bladders, and repair of muscle damage. Many of the

WOUNDED WARRIORS

One of the great challenges facing the governments of the United States and Canada is treating soldiers who have suffered disabling injuries in combat zones.

Researchers at the Massachusetts Institute of Technology's Lincoln Laboratory's Technology Office Innovation Laboratory (TOIL) have been working to improve the quality of prosthetic devices—**custom medical devices** built to fit a patient—that are available to open-source groups such as e-Nable. According to a story at 3dprint.com, "They are developing ways to offer better finger motion, add non-electronic temperature and tactile feedback, and add motor technology to new designs."

Among the groups the researchers are hoping to help is the Wounded Warrior Project. The researchers are developing a way to tell people wearing a prosthetic hand how hard they are gripping something.

E-Nable shares designs for 3D-printed prostheses so they can be custom made at a lower cost and much more quickly than if the wounded veteran had to go through proper medical channels at the Department of Veterans Affairs.

Retired Army Captain Jonathan Pruden, himself a wounded warrior, told Congress about the problems facing the almost 1,300 service members who had lost at least one limb in Iraq or Afghanistan as of March 2012. "I personally know warriors who stay home from our events, stay home from school and from work, don't play ball with their kids, or live in chronic pain while they wait for a new prosthesis," Captain Pruden said on May 16, 2012.

For members of the Wounded Warrior Project, 3D printing can quickly bring a return to a somewhat normal life.

projects are related to treatment for wounded warriors, US veterans who have been injured in the line of duty. According to WFIRM, a considerable amount of the research there is related to the Wounded Warrior Project, which helps provide treatment for injured veterans. The Armed Forces Institute of Regenerative Medicine is related to WFIRM.

Modern medicine has brought about a higher survival rate for veterans who sustain complex injuries on the battlefield. This includes surviving injuries such as the loss of limbs. The goal of research at centers like WFIRM is to improve the quality of care overall by engaging with the body's natural healing ability with help from 3D printing technologies.

On a personal note, I have repeatedly witnessed in clinic the effect of war on patients, whether from a rifle blast or a machete to the face. The results can be devastating, with a long and profound impact on the veteran and patient's quality of life. 3D printing for tissue and body regeneration holds a great deal of promise for a medical care revolution.

We have discussed many new and exciting technologies that have emerged from 3D printing due to its nature as a gateway technology. This is a rare example of how one gateway technology can produce a second gateway technology, i.e., biological printing. The options available to doctors in the present and future will permit them to increase the customization and thus the safety of the treatments offered to patients, as we will see in the next section.

Advanced Concepts

We have covered a lot of the technology involved in customizing wound repair care for an explosives blast. If we consider the processing pipeline in this particularly complex scenario, the first step, according to WFIRM, is to scan the injury. This form of input gives us a topographical map of the structure of the patient's unique wound.

This scan, which can be described as a three-dimensional wave, can then be imported into a CAD software program for editing and for treatment. Once the correct model is established, it can be sent to the computer for further adjustment in a CAD program. This information can then be sent to the 3D printer that directly treats the wounds. These techniques use surface topography, wavelength science, surface difference analysis, and mapping.

The laser scanner is reading the rugged terrain of the explosives wound like a topographical map of a mountain range. The key areas to avoid for the care provider would be to watch out for any undercuts. Once the surface is read, it can then be described by the software program as a three-dimensional wavelength (remember x, y, and z). The difference between how the surface of the wound looks beforehand, and how the team would like it to look after, is a comparison of two different surfaces, and this will provide how best to modify the printed tissue.

Teams like the one at WFIRM require a broad set of skills and a diversity of team members' professions. This is because the medical problems being treated are often very complex, not least from an anatomical standpoint. The team includes medical doctors (MDs), scientists with PhDs and masters' degrees, and many other support staff. The degrees needed to become involved all require STEM and STEAM coursework.

This is another example of a challenging and rewarding career that requires patience and attention to your STEAM classes. It does take diligence and hard work, but the payoff is both financially and personally rewarding. As a care provider, I can attest to how rewarding it is to make a constructive difference in the life of someone else in your daily career.

Surgery

As a patient is prepared for surgery, the surgical team has many things to consider. The surgeon approaches the surgery with the knowledge that things may not go as planned. One variable that is reduced by 3D printing is the mystery of each patient's unique anatomy. An example can be seen in the treatment of patients with head and neck cancer.

In nature and in life, our anatomy generally remains hidden. This presents a challenge when there is an injury to our bodies, such as our skulls, that requires treatment. Historically, surgeons often approached procedures in the operating room without knowing the condition of a patient's anatomy underneath. The patients and their families often did not understand quite what was happening, or what would happen, to their bodies.

Medical diagnostic imaging allows for a 2D image of the patient's anatomy, whether it is a printed document, such as an X-ray, or an image projected on a screen, such as CT imaging software. This ability to visualize can also lead to new diagnoses by showing problems or illnesses that may not be visible otherwise. After I accidentally swallowed a penny as a child, you could see the face of Abraham Lincoln clear as day on the X-ray film. It was in my lower intestine (the penny, not the film).

The power of 3D printing for surgical treatment comes into play when the surgeon can walk into a hospital room with a model of the patient's skull in his or her hand. The surgeon can then explain both the patient's condition and what will be done during the procedure, such as removal of a tumor. This will often reduce the patient's anxiety going into surgery, as the patient will have a clearer idea of what part of his or her body is going to be changed by the surgery.

Printing an anatomical model can also reduce time in the operating room because the surgeon also has a clearer idea of what is happening beneath the surface. This is especially important for the human skull, as it encases our brains. Without a model, the surgeon has to make informed guesses under high pressure, increasing the risk of human error. The cost of error in surgery is always high, both in terms of quality of life and dollars. Therefore the development and use of 3D technology in surgical treatment has led to a reduction in surgical errors and resulted in an improvement in the quality of life for patients and their families.

The options for a career in medicine using 3D technology are many: surgeon, technologist, prosthetist, 3D software engineer, 3D printer specialist, consultant on the overlap of these fields. All of these people are involved in improving the quality of life for the patient by creating accurate representations of the insides of our bodies using 3D printing technology.

All of these options relate to the visualization of a patient's anatomy. There are many other areas in which 3D printing can make a difference in surgical outcomes, including the production of customized tools. There are fields of medicine that require very specific tools, and because surgical tools are often mass-produced, the tools may not fit the patient's anatomy. This means the tool really is unfit for the job, and a solution must be found.

There is an opportunity for surgical improvement by creating customized tools for working on an individual. As we have established, humans are not one size fits all, and each of our bodies is different. It therefore makes sense that surgeons may need more particular tools to suit specialized tasks, such as for neurosurgery and pediatric cardiovascular procedures. Surgeons have advanced anatomical knowledge and can coordinate with a technologist or engineer to produce the tools that they need, without having to work through a factory (which would not be cheap!).

Education

In chapter 2, we discussed how each of us experiences the world in a slightly different way, and as a result, we all learn differently. Some of us retain information, such as directions to a friend's house, best when we hear it over the phone, while some of us need it written down. Others need a map (or a map app!) to see where the home is in relation to familiar streets and parks. The first group would be "verbal" learners, and the second "visual." This diversity is one of the many challenges facing today's educators.

One strong value of 3D printing to education is engagement. By providing opportunities for students to explore in ways they could not before, this technology permits educators to empower their students to engage their unique learning styles by exploring the world in different ways. By using 3D technology, students can view and even print models of vases made by ancient cultures, or explore the microscopic universe.

The phrase "a picture is worth a thousand words" is used to convey the power of 2D imaging. Consequently, 3D imaging or the production of models using 3D manufacturing allows the student to experience a topic verbally, visually, and by touch. These printers and technologies permit a range of options for teaching students with diverse abilities and ways of understanding their world.

More and more public institutions are making access to these technologies available to the public with the goal of improving learning, understanding, and knowledge of the world around us. Public libraries increasingly have learning labs where anyone can go in and receive instruction on how to use 3D software or print a model of their choice. This accessibility allows people who have invention ideas or who simply want to try it out to become savvy with 3D technology. Most important, it empowers people with the ability to teach themselves new technology.

One aspect of this sharing of information that we touched upon when discussing the maker movement is how it can empower people with information. "Knowledge is power" as the saying goes, and one aspect of 3D printing is that it can be expensive. This may preclude some people of lower socioeconomic status, both nationally and globally, from gaining access to certain 3D technologies.

However, via education, the internet, the open-source community, and the maker movement, CAD programs and additive manufacturing technologies such as FDM have become increasingly accessible to people, especially students, regardless of income. With that being said, there is some cynicism regarding the value of some low-cost printers, if there is a loss of quality.

The Digitization Program Office at the Smithsonian Institution and Smithsonian X 3D are archiving their collection, from photographs stored at the National Gallery of Art, to pre-Columbian artifacts and sculptures. Using scanners and modeling software, they have made irreplaceable items deeply important to our culture available to all of us. Something that was made painstakingly by hand thousands of years ago can be reproduced in a school or public library for a very low cost using stereolithography or FDM.

In considering what career you may be interested in, if you like the idea of teaching, 3D printing presents the opportunity for a lot of fun at your work. Using the models mentioned above, you can take your class on a tour of the world, and they can leave at the end of the day with a keepsake that will also help them remember the

There are hundreds of different types of 3D technology devices, and they are used in a multitude of new professions.

topic. Creating an emotional connection and providing a physical memory can strike a chord with students and is a great way to connect and inspire them in a given topic.

If you'd like to become a college professor, it is a delightful experience to watch your students' knowledge of 3D technology grow beyond what you have taught them. Using the method of understanding that I mentioned in the previous chapters, I have seen students go on to create models of living rooms, ships, and even watches. To see them go from mild boredom to total engagement and independent work is very rewarding.

Tinkercad has been an especially useful program for me as an instructor. It offers simple lessons and tutorials, and has a sense of humor, such as celebrations when a lesson is completed. Most important, it offers a gentle introduction to the sometimes convoluted world of computer drafting. The environment in Tinkercad is relatively stable, meaning that the user does not feel as though he or she is flying around in space. When I was quickly moving through a more advanced program during a tutorial, a mature student jokingly claimed to have motion sickness because of how dynamic the viewpoint had become.

Tinkercad is also brightly and engagingly colored, which is of great help in a subject that, especially for creative types, can be a little dry. The program turns learning into a game, which is always a great and engaging approach. And the programmers incorporated a lot of humor into the software as well. This is a very valuable teaching tool, hence my rampant use of cows and lasers as teaching tools in this book.

One of the best features of the program is how someone with little to no computer literacy can go from zero experience with 3D printing to being able to create a 3D print within an afternoon. Tinkercad automates and streamlines the file preparing process by limiting the ways the user can produce an object and by making the file prep process point and click. This simplicity, especially with the proper supervision, can generate an enormous amount of confidence in a student after she or he prints a first object. This is even more true for older students with lower levels of computer literacy.

Itzhak Perlman is one of the world's best violin players, and his teacher was Ivan Galamian, who taught many other prestigious and famous musicians. Galamian's approach was to teach to the student– to recognize the student's particular strengths and weaknesses, and to adapt the lessons and teaching method accordingly. Until then, music instruction and many other areas of teaching were insistent by tradition on a uniform approach. This did not leave a great deal of room for learning differences. Galamian was, as you can see, not only correct but very successful in the caliber of student that he produced.

My approach as an educator and instructor is the same, incorporating the metacognitive approach, and time and time again I have seen good results because, as a teacher, you are not trying to put a square peg in a round hole. You are adapting to the circumstances presented to you, and in doing so, you are acknowledging that you are teaching a human being with his or her own individual needs, not a robot. If you would like to become an educator or teacher and use 3D printing, then I recommend the use of instruction tools that engage the imagination of the student, as the subject material can be a little technical, albeit exhilarating in effect. Tinkercad is a perfect example of an effective tool for engaging the imagination of the real as well as the inner child that you are teaching.

This customization and engagement is not limited to Tinkercad. Many other programs are starting to recognize the value of simplicity in controls and more visual engagement, such as color. While you or I may be very comfortable in the digital environment, computers can be intimidating to those who have not become immersed in them. This is even more true of 3D printing, which has developed a bit of mystery and magic to it due to excellent PR. Your job as the educator is to draw back the curtain and show students how everything works. To see the "Ah hah! I get it!" moment in a student's eyes is very rewarding.

Tinkercad is also of value not just for basic instruction but as a first step in providing teaching in more complex programs such as Rhino. Rhino can be a very logical program if introduced correctly, or it can be visually overwhelming to the unindoctrinated. I have hinted at how, like Adobe Photoshop, Rhino can be very big and easy to get lost in. However, if you use the teaching and learning methods described in this book, especially the processing pipeline, and if you introduce advanced software in concert with a simple program like Tinkercad or SketchUp, it is easy for your students to become 3D printing rock stars in no time.

Conclusion

Over the course of this book, we have covered the fundamentals of 3D printing beginner processes, including the types of 3D printing available today, among them emerging and sustaining technologies. These technology categories included vat polymerization, material extrusion, powder bed fusion (PBF), sheet lamination, **directed energy deposition,** concrete and stone construction printing, biotechnology, and 4D printing.

These categories were explored in depth, including historical development, inventors, pros and cons of the different features of the technology, and future outlooks. Concrete examples of what can be produced by the tech were given (literally in some cases) to assist in instruction and memorization of the reading content. The evolution of "the family tree" of technologies was presented to show how the development of one process, such as stereolithography, or STL, affected later technologies, such as selective laser sintering (SLS). We also discussed lasers as they related to our ancient ancestors and the future of space exploration.

We have also covered how to approach learning the processing pipeline shared by much of 3D technology, and we have learned it from a metacognitive, or "30,000-foot," view, as well as considering each step in detail. This included concrete examples of how people in different professions would use the technologies at each step of the pipeline. You are now in a better position to learn more in depth about different types of 3D printing based on your understanding of the processing pipeline.

Learning about the processing pipeline led to a survey of the different types of careers available that use or engage with 3D printing, and how to best prepare for them. This includes learning different STEM and STEAM curricula, such as art, math (including algebra and geometry), and physics. The usefulness of these classes in the range of professions highlighted the need for new and properly educated or trained students for the range of job openings currently available in 3D printing. The jobs are waiting, but it is essential to get the proper knowledge and understanding first.

With that training, there is a sea of fields with fascinating careers ranging from the fine arts (making sculptures to be seen in galleries), to engineering (designing and building the engines of rockets for space exploration), to medicine (including surgical treatment of head injuries and repairing organs with custom tissue engineering). We also discussed opportunities in reinventing the technologies themselves, as well as the software.

All of this was presented in the form of deep history, an approach that helps define our role as students, as human beings engaged in a long tradition of innovation, and, especially, as Americans. It is in our blood to seek out knowledge, to challenge the status quo, and hopefully find treasure in the process. I hope that you will continue to expand your understanding of 3D technology and its promise for tomorrow.

GLOSSARY

acquisition The input of data by various methods into a computer.

additive manufacturing Another term for 3D printing, this is the method of creating objects by adding material one layer at a time.

anaplastologist A person who makes prosthetic replacements for missing, malformed, or damaged parts on a critical place on the face or body.

biotechnology AM An additive manufacturing process that incorporates the use of biological materials to print living tissue structures to replace damaged or missing tissue.

CAD/CAM An acronym that stands for "computer-aided design" and "computer-aided manufacturing." An umbrella term that is used to describe a large number of technologies involved in the processing pipeline. CAD allows for the creation of images in three dimensions, and CAM involves cutting away materials using drills and lathes directed by computers reading instructions written by CAD.

cathode A charged electrode that directs the passage of electrons.

custom medical devices Approved medical devices made to the specifications of an individual patient.

directed energy deposition Additive manufacturing processes that use energy transference (such as via laser or electron gun) to alter material in a sequential manner for fabrication of parts.

electron gun An instrument for controlling and producing a beam of electrons using a heated cathode.

emerging technology Technologies that through targeted development will or are capable of creating social change.

extracellular matrix A collection of molecules secreted by a cell that provide structural and biochemical support for the surrounding cells. The matrix is the non-cellular portion of the tissue.

4D printing The fabrication of 3D printed parts that self-assemble over time through knowledge of geometry and material science.

gateway technology A technology that will create social and environmental change by making the invention of new technologies possible.

innovate To introduce new ideas or technologies that challenge the status quo.

landmark A structure that is easily recognized. Landmark surface analysis is a method of scientific investigation that uses recognizable features on one or more similar objects to create measurements.

laser An instrument that uses concentrated light that is created by the excitation of photons using mirrors.

medical illustration A visual translation of complex medical or biological information to be used in patient education and medical research.

monomer A type of chemical with a simple molecular structure.

ocularist A person who makes and fits artificial eyes.

organ printing Using 3D printing to create an artificial device for transplanting or study.

polymer A chemical composed of monomers grouped together as one molecule.

powder bed fusion A group of manufacturing technologies that use particle material and directed energy and/or chemicals to fuse the particles and create objects via layering.

processing pipeline A recipe for creating a 3D-printed object, whose steps include input, processing, output, and finishing.

rapid prototyping A type of additive manufacturing in which products are 3D printed and tested for form and function. This allows for quick changes to be made in a product, which can again be printed and tested.

scaffolding A structure that holds biological material together until it can develop and stand on its own.

spectrophotometry The measurement of the interaction of light with a given material or substance using a spectrophotometer.

STEAM An acronym that stands for "STEM" plus the inclusion of "art and design." STEAM initiatives focus on the equal value of art and design as education initiatives by themselves and in relation to other fields.

STEM An acronym that stands for "science, engineering, technology, and math," and is used in reference to those fields as well as describing education initiatives focusing on them.

stereolithography The creation of objects from a liquid polymer using the process of photopolymerization via lasers or light and the sequential deposition of material.

stereophotogrammetry A method of scientific investigation that uses photography via multiple cameras to record different angles of a given object. These photographs are then combined to produce a 3D representation of the object.

sustaining technology A technology that has become commonplace in usage and has often become required in a given profession, e.g., laptop computers. May also refer to nondisruptive changes in existing technology.

3D printing Also known as additive manufacturing (AM); the fabrication of parts by sequential deposition of layers of material.

tissue engineering The combination and use of cells and artificial materials to create designed solutions for problems with biological tissues, as well as with the goal of mimicking biological tissues.

vat polymerization The fabrication of an object using a light-sensitive resin that is sequentially exposed to light in order to harden and build on itself.

workflow The series of steps that are used to create a given result, such as a 3D-printed object.

ziggurat A temple tower from ancient Mesopotamia that is pyramidal and built in stages

FURTHER INFORMATION

Books

Cline, Lydia. *3D Printing with Autodesk 123D, Tinkercad, and MakerBot.* New York: McGraw-Hill Education, 2014.

Fisher, Gordon. *Blender 3D Printing Essentials.* Birmingham, UK: Packt Publishing, 2013.

Hovarth, Joan. *Mastering 3D Printing: Modeling, Printing, and Prototyping with RepRap-Style 3D Printers.* New York: Apress, 2014.

Kloski, Lisa Wallach, and Nick Kloski. *Getting Started with 3D Printing: A Hands-On Guide to the Hardware, Software, and Services Behind the New Manufacturing Revolution.* San Francisco: Maker Media, Inc., 2016.

Mongeon, Bridgette. *3D Technology in Fine Art and Craft: Exploring 3D Printing, Scanning, Sculpting, and Milling.* Burlington, MA: Focal Press, 2016.

Organizations

MakerBot's Thingiverse

https://www.thingiverse.com

An open-source community for sharing thousands of 3D print designs.

STEM to STEAM

http://stemtosteam.org

The Rhode Island School of Design champions the synergy between the arts and technology in an effort to "influence employers to hire artists and designers to drive innovation." There are links to the latest stories and videos on the subject.

3D Warehouse: SketchUp

https://3Dwarehouse.sketchup.com

This clearinghouse provides free digital 3D models that you can download and import into programs such as Rhino and Tinkercad.

Videos

4D Printing: Cube Self-Folding Strand

https://vimeo.com/58840897

Learn how a printer builds functionality directly into materials to produce a product that behaves like a robot but doesn't require complex electromechanical devices.

What If 3D Printing Was 100x Faster?

https://www.ted.com/talks/joe_desimone_what_if_3d_printing_was_25x_faster

Joseph DeSimone delivers a TED talk in 2015 on CLIP, a new, fast 3D printing technique that was inspired by *Terminator 2*.

Websites

Loughborough University Additive Manufacturing Research Group

http://www.lboro.ac.uk/research/amrg/about

A globally recognized leader in AM research and education; an excellent reference website with clear educational videos.

Make Magazine

http://makezine.com

The web resource for the maker community and *Make* magazine.

Massachusetts Institute of Technology (MIT) Self-Assembly Lab 4D Printing

http://www.selfassemblylab.net/4DPrinting.php

This cross-disciplinary research lab at MIT investigates what it calls "self-assembly and programmable material technologies aimed at reimagining construction, manufacturing, product assembly and performance."

Rhinoceros

http://www.rhino3D.com

This company is a leader in the field of computer modeling and 3D printing software design.

Tinkercad

https://www.tinkercad.com

Tinkercad is a great entry point for learning 3D design.

INDEX

Page numbers in **boldface** are illustrations. Entries in **boldface** are glossary terms.

ABOUT THE AUTHOR

Michael E. Degnan, MSc, BFA, first saw the life-changing applications of 3D printing in prosthetic treatment of patients with a facial difference during his training at the Johns Hopkins School of Medicine and King's College London, in England. Degnan has consulted on the use of, advised on curriculum for, and taught courses for college and professional development on the use of 3D technologies. He also regularly presents on translating 3D technology for the everyday user, including at the Smithsonian Institution. Degnan likes to use emerging technologies (such as the 3Doodler pen) in his fine arts practice, based in New York State.